NATIONAL MUSEUM OF DANCE

National Museum of Dance

National Museum of Dance

AND HALL OF FAME

Celebrating 30 Years

LISA SCHLANSKER KOLOSEK

excelsior editions

Book design, Laura DiRado

Published by
State University of New York Press, Albany

Excelsior Editions is an imprint of State University of New York Press

For information, contact
State University of New York Press, Albany, NY
www.sunypress.edu

Production, Laurie D. Searl
Marketing, Fran Keneston

Kolosek, Lisa Schlansker, (date)
    National Museum of Dance and Hall of Fame: Celebrating 30 Years
    ISBN 9781438467450

Library of Congress Control Number: 2017934257

10 9 8 7 6 5 4 3 2 1

PAGE ii:
Aerial view of the Washington Baths, circa 1920.

PAGE vi:
Vintage postcard from the Washington Baths, circa 1920s.

PAGE 272:
Madonna (1995) by Andrew DeVries, bronze, from the 2013 exhibition, *Homage to Dance*.

THIS BOOK IS DEDICATED TO

THE FOUNDERS OF THE

NATIONAL MUSEUM OF DANCE

AND HALL OF FAME

Contents

VIII

Mark Morris

Artistic Director/Choreographer, Mark Morris Dance Group

Dance has a longer history than almost any other human activity. Why was there no Dance Museum before this one? Didn't anyone notice that we needed one? Well, here it is, and it is selective, quirky, and marvelous: The National Museum of Dance and Hall of Fame in Saratoga Springs, New York.

The building itself looks a lot like a mausoleum and feels like a sanitarium because of its history and location. Thankfully, the tone and the taste of the collection is warm and friendly and, crucially, serious. Dancers, choreographers, writers, critics, trends, and history are represented and presented. The collections and exhibits are not exhaustive, but specific and varied and engaging.

Dance as an old, strange form of social activity, art form, theater performance, communication, re-creation, personal experience, show business, time killer, workout, the sacred and the profane. Dance deserves our curious attention and reverence. What was there before dance? Language, agriculture, the wheel, fire? Sex, certainly. I imagine that dancing started when our wonderful ancestrals decided to run toward something instead of away from it. Dancing occurred just after noticing the heartbeat, and thereby rhythm. So much dancing in the whole world is a result and response to mystery, physical labor, storytelling, celebration, boredom, entertainment, communication, and glamour. Watch. Listen. Repeat.

We who work behind the scenes and in the public domain to present dance and music to the interested public, love and value everyone who has led up to the now of dance. The history of dancing is a long one. It is fascinating and deep. So many points of view, techniques, opinions, lineages, studies, stories, ballets, spectacles, pageants, competitions, conventions, movements, theories, delights, for all of us. Always interesting. Always more to learn.

My own life has ever been a dancing life and I think I know a little something about it by now. In fact, it's all I know. I've got it. I can read it. I get bored of it. I despair of it. I have faith in it. I admire it. I worship and resent it. I am a choreographer of dances and have lived with my own dance company since 1980. I am so grateful to have been inducted into the museum along with so many notable and important people in the world of dance. And what a wonderful compliment! How nice to be taken as seriously as I take my responsibility to this incredible and untranslatable art form. I have no doubt that the long, vast history of dance will continue as long as the civilization it honors. This book is a good story about a great place to visit. Hail Terpsichore! Hail National Museum of Dance and Hall of Fame!

FACING PAGE:
Mark Morris, Artistic Director/Choreographer, Mark Morris Dance Group.

INTRODUCTION

Raul P. Martinez

Director, National Museum of Dance and School of the Arts

Thirty years ago, a bold and ambitious plan was realized to create the only museum in this country dedicated exclusively to the art form of dance. In June 1987, the National Museum of Dance and Hall of Fame officially opened its doors in the meticulously restored Washington Baths, a historic 1920s bathhouse in Saratoga Springs, New York. The story of this Museum is captivating and unique, and represents the important history of Saratoga Springs itself, which includes a long tradition of dance and an even longer tradition of health, with an abundance of world-renowned mineral springs found right in our own backyard.

As we celebrate and reflect on three remarkable decades of this cultural institution, we are reminded of the steadfast commitment of our founders and their families, as well as board members, staff, volunteers, and the dance community at large, both local and global. We are energized by our tremendous legacy—the history of our building and our founding, our wide-ranging roster of exhibitions and programming, our singular and evolving collection, the development of our Lewis A. Swyer Studios, and the transformation and growth of our School of the Arts—all of which is expressed in this beautiful book. We are also reminded of our incredible resilience. Despite a strong measure of success, the Museum, in fact,

endured years of financial uncertainty and administrative flux. As a result, our reputation was compromised and our viability questioned. The good news is, however, that we're still here and we're thriving. More than fourteen thousand visitors come to the Museum each year to experience compelling exhibitions; live dance, theater, and music performances in our studios and in the Mr. and Mrs. Ronald A. Riggi Theater; and inspiring arts education initiatives such as master classes and discussions with celebrated choreographers and dancers. Vital collaborations within our local community and within the dance community remain a priority.

We continue to be ambitious at the Museum and the School of the Arts as we strive to make dance and its interesting and surprising history both inclusive and widely accessible. In doing so, we hope to reach and cultivate new and diverse audiences to ensure the future of this magnificent art form. We invite you to explore our history in these pages and to engage with us at the Museum through our extraordinary exhibitions and dynamic programming. Welcome to the National Museum of Dance and Hall of Fame.

FACING PAGE:
Raul P. Martinez, Director, National Museum of Dance and School of the Arts.

CHAPTER ONE

Founding the National Museum of Dance and Hall of Fame

The rich history of the National Museum of Dance and Hall of Fame began with a long-held, highly ambitious idea developed by Lewis A. Swyer, general contractor and chairman of the Saratoga Performing Arts Center (SPAC), one of the country's most vibrant summer dance and music festivals. In the early 1980s, the New York State Office of Parks, Recreation, and Historic Preservation, led by Commissioner Orin Lehman, initiated a feasibility study and actively sought proposals for the reuse of the historic Washington Baths located within the Saratoga Spa State Park and within walking distance of SPAC. In 1984, together with SPAC's president and executive director Herb Chesbrough, Swyer presented his concept to philanthropist and dance enthusiast Marylou Whitney at her Cady Hill estate in Saratoga Springs. Mrs. Whitney immediately embraced and supported the idea and the three submitted a proposal to establish the first hall of fame and museum of dance in the United States. The Dansmuseet in Stockholm, Sweden, the only other dance museum in the world, was founded in 1953 by Rolf de Maré, director of the avant-garde Ballets Suédois.

FACING PAGE:
Lewis A. Swyer, Marylou Whitney, and Herb Chesbrough at the May 12, 1986 press conference to introduce the Museum.

FOUNDING THE NATIONAL MUSEUM OF DANCE AND HALL OF FAME

By the mid-1980s, Saratoga Springs had become a hub for both ballet and modern dance, and therefore, Swyer, Whitney, and Chesbrough considered it an ideal location for such a venture. The opening of SPAC in 1966, with the New York City Ballet (NYCB) as its founding resident dance company, was pivotal in creating a culture and audience of and for dance in the region, with Saratoga Springs at the epicenter. For twenty years, NYCB had been performing masterworks from their repertory for four weeks in July, with eight new works receiving world premieres at SPAC.[1] George Balanchine, founder and ballet master of NYCB, had tremendous admiration and respect for Saratoga Springs and believed its audiences should experience the same caliber of work found at Lincoln Center. As SPAC was in development in the early 1960s, so too was the Capital Area Modern Dance Council (CAMDC). Formed in 1963, CAMDC brought some of the most influential modern dance companies to the region to perform and conduct master classes, including the Tamiris-Nagrin Dance Company, Erick Hawkins Dance, Paul Taylor Dance Company, and Paul Sanasardo Dance Company. In 1969, CAMDC was newly headquartered at the Spa Little Theater in the Saratoga Spa State Park. Under the programming umbrella of SPAC, CAMDC offered a four-week summer school of modern dance led by choreographer Paul Sanasardo and initiated a festival that would present modern dance concerts by trailblazing companies such as Alvin Ailey, Murray Louis, Twyla Tharp, and José Limón.[2] Notable summer dance intensives located in Saratoga Springs further underscored the city as a focal point for dance in these early years. With the encouragement of Balanchine, the Briansky Saratoga Ballet Center was founded in 1965 by celebrated dancers Oleg Briansky and Mireille Briane. It welcomed students from around the country and the world for some forty-seven years. The New York State Summer School of the Arts (NYSSSA) School of Ballet was founded in 1976 and housed at Skidmore College.[3] NYSSSA's School of Dance would subsequently be established in 1989. Skidmore College began to create its own dance program in the late 1960s, thus enabling it to host these summer intensives and various influential guest artists.[4] The city's reputation as a dance community was no doubt bolstered by the presence of newly retired NYCB principal dancer Melissa Hayden, a Skidmore faculty member from 1973 to 1976. In addition, proximity to Jacob's Pillow Dance Festival in Becket, Massachusetts, added in part to the development of Saratoga Springs as a dance destination with artists and audiences traveling between these two centers.

LEFT AND RIGHT:
George Balanchine with Susan Pilarre and Colleen Neary at the July 15, 1977 George Balanchine Day parade in downtown Saratoga Springs. BALANCHINE is a Trademark of The George Balanchine Trust.

Dancer on a temporary stage at the George Balanchine Day parade in downtown Saratoga Springs, July 15, 1977.

New York State ultimately determined Saratoga Springs to be an excellent spot for this proposed cultural institution. In July 1984, the Department of Parks, Recreation, and Historic Preservation awarded the newly incorporated National Museum of Dance and Hall of Fame a twenty-year lease of the Washington Baths and its ten-acre site in the Saratoga Spa State Park, with the option for a twenty-year extension, at an annual cost of one dollar.

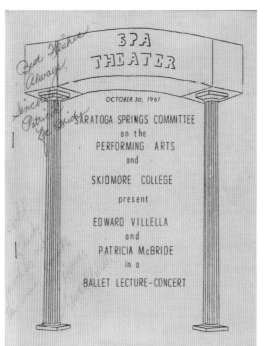

FACING PAGE:
Oleg Briansky teaching ballet class at the Briansky Saratoga Ballet Center, circa 1960. Gift of Oleg Briansky.

LEFT:
Mireille Briane and George Balanchine in Saratoga Springs on George Balanchine Day, July 15, 1977. BALANCHINE is a Trademark of The George Balanchine Trust.

RIGHT:
Program signed by Patricia McBride and Edward Villella from an October 30, 1961, Ballet Lecture-Concert at the Spa Theater, presented by the Saratoga Springs Committee on the Performing Arts and Skidmore College. This concert was integral in promoting the development of SPAC.

Washington Baths

The effervescent mineral waters distinct to Saratoga Springs have been in regular use as a health curative through drinking and bathing since the end of the eighteenth century. Over the course of the nineteenth century, Saratoga Springs became a popular and fashionable destination for health seekers to "take the cure." At the same time, the privately owned mineral springs were increasingly exploited for commercial profit, including the manufacture of carbonated beverages. To prevent the continued overextraction of carbonic acid, a process that significantly depleted water levels and the therapeutic value of the waters, legislation was written in 1909 that allowed New York State to purchase the vast majority of the mineral springs and wells in the city. The Saratoga Springs Commission and the State Reservation at Saratoga Springs were created to preserve and protect the waters and make them available for public use.[5] To this end, four new bathhouses were planned for the State Reservation, much of which became the Saratoga Spa State Park in 1962.

The Washington Baths were established in a turn-of-the-century structure originally built for the Natural Carbonic Gas Company, which in the 1910s was leased to fine furnituremaker Saratoga Wood Craftsmen, Inc. The renovation and reconstruction of the building for the Washington Baths, designed by the state architect of New York, Lewis F. Pilcher,

FACING PAGE:
Front drive of the Washington Baths, 1931.
RIGHT:
Entrance to the Washington Baths, 1934.

began in October 1918. A heating plant was also constructed on the property that year that would control not only the steam and electric power to the adjacent Washington and Lincoln Baths but also the massive supply of mineral water. This building corresponded stylistically to the Washington Baths. The first wing was opened to the public for use during the last two weeks of August 1919 and was fully operational for the 1920 season.

In its heyday, the Washington Baths rivaled the great therapeutic spas of Europe. The H-shaped building boasted eighty-four semiprivate and twenty-four private rooms in two wings, one for men and the other for women. The resplendent, light-filled Beaux Arts foyer housed the reception area and offices for the superintendent and the medical staff. This state-of-the-art spa offered both hydrotherapy and mechanotherapy including a range of cabinet treatments, colonic irrigation, Turkish baths, massage, salt and alcohol rubs, cardiac therapy, and infrared treatments, in addition to the widely prescribed mineral baths. Terraces in the front and back of the bath house allowed patients to rest and take the "sun cure." After nearly sixty years in operation, the Washington Baths closed in the summer of 1978 due to a widespread decline in the use of mineral waters for health, wellness, and rehabilitation.

RIGHT:
Bottled Saratoga Geyser mineral water.
FACING PAGE, CLOCKWISE FROM TOP LEFT:
The northeast terrace of the Washington Baths.
Patients taking the "sun cure" on the back terrace.
A private treatment room including a mineral bath tub.
Cabinet treatments.

SITE CONCEPT for the
NATIONAL MUSEUM
OF DANCE
SARATOGA SPRINGS, NEW YORK
PREPARED BY THE SARATOGA ASSOCIATES
LANDSCAPE ARCHITECTS · ARCHITECTS · PLANNERS

Development of the Dream

The founding mission of the National Museum of Dance and Hall of Fame was "to cultivate, promote, foster, sponsor, and develop among its members and the community at large, the appreciation, understanding, taste, and love of the Musical Arts, especially the Dance; to create a National Hall of Fame for the advancement of such purposes; to secure the interest of the patrons of these Arts, and to promote and encourage the study of these Arts and the history thereof and provide the means for popular instruction and enjoyment thereof."[6] The overarching idea was that all forms of dance were to be honored and that the Museum should be living, with dancers taking class and choreographers creating new work right on the property. This mission translated into a three-phase plan developed by the founding board of directors, each phase to be completed as funds were raised.

Phase One included the restoration and enhancement of the foyer, which would house one of four exhibitions in a 1986 preview season and become the permanent home of the Mr. and Mrs. Cornelius Vanderbilt Whitney Hall of Fame beginning in 1987. The renovation and construction of two 5,000 square foot galleries on either side of the foyer was also included in first phase, as well as the building of administrative offices and the museum shop. Phase Two called for the construction of a one hundred-seat theater for lectures and film screenings in the southeast section of the Museum. A library and resource center with individual study rooms were to be built in the Museum's northeast wing.[7] Phase Three was reserved for the construction of a separate building behind

FACING PAGE:
Museum founders Mr. and Mrs. Cornelius Vanderbilt Whitney and Lewis A. Swyer at the May 12, 1986 press conference.

LEFT:
Museum brochure from the 1986 preview season.

RIGHT:
The Museum's first director, Alison Moore, at the 1986 press conference.

the Museum to house three state-of-the-art dance studios, reflective of the dimensions of NYCB's stage at Lincoln Center.[8] The intent was for Museum visitors to view professional dance training and live performance, and to provide a home for NYSSSA's Schools of Ballet and Dance. Plans beyond the first three phases included a dance therapy facility within the Museum in which mineral water could be accessed and utilized for rehabilitation, a sculpture garden, and a full, removable stage situated among grassy, graduated levels behind the Museum that could accommodate an audience of up to five hundred for outdoor performances of dance and music.

The founding board of the Museum was comprised almost entirely of SPAC board members with the full intention that the Museum and SPAC would operate in close collaboration with one another, including shared advertising and public relations, and initial directorship of the Hall of Fame.[9] It was decided that Lewis A. Swyer would serve as chairman, Marylou Whitney as president, Herb Chesbrough as executive vice president, Nancy Norman Lassalle as secretary, and Jacob Schulman as treasurer, in addition to William E. Murray, W. Barnabas McHenry, Gordon Ambach, Orin Lehman-Ex Officio, and Cornelius Vanderbilt Whitney-Ex Officio. The board of directors expanded at once to include SPAC trustee Lillian Phipps and Charles V. Wait. Through its affiliation with SPAC and board member Nancy Norman Lassalle, the Museum was somewhat inherently connected to NYCB at the outset. Lassalle served on the boards of SPAC, NYCB, and the School of American Ballet and

was involved with several exhibitions showcasing NYCB at the Museum between 1988 and 1999. She has remained a presence on the Museum's board throughout its history and her legacy is manifest.[10] So too is the tremendous legacy of the Whitney and Swyer families who have served on the board from its inception.[11]

Since 2005, current president of the board Michele Riggi has guided the National Museum of Dance with great vision and acumen. Through her extraordinary generosity, the founders' original three-phase plan was completed with the construction of the Mr. and Mrs. Ronald A. Riggi Theater in the northwest wing of the Museum in 2014. The forty-eight-seat black box theater hosts film screenings and lectures, as well as opera, music, comedy, drama, and dance performances, and counts The Creative Place International as its resident theater company.

FACING PAGE, CLOCKWISE FROM TOP LEFT:
Anne and Lewis Swyer.

Marylou Whitney at the 1986 press conference.

Nancy Norman Lassalle and Merce Cunningham at his June 20, 1993 induction into the Hall of Fame. Cunningham's stained glass award was designed and made by the artist Hope Hawthorne.

Herb Chesbrough at the 1986 press conference.

LEFT:
Michele and Ron Riggi at the grand unveiling of the Mr. and Mrs. Ronald A. Riggi Theater, July 24, 2014.

Reconstruction

The lease agreement with the State of New York stipulated that the Museum was to be responsible for the complete renovation, operation, and maintenance of the Washington Baths building. The project budget for the three-phase plan was estimated at between $3.5 and $5 million, all of which was to be raised through private donors. Mr. and Mrs. Cornelius Vanderbilt Whitney were the lead funders, contributing a total of $650,000 by 1986. Founding board member William E. Murray and board chairman Lewis A. Swyer were the other major funders at this stage.

Swyer was one of the region's most prominent builders, responsible for SPAC, the Edward Durell Stone–designed First Unitarian Society Church in Schenectady, and a number of Albany's landmarks. He was also a stalwart patron of the arts as chairman of SPAC and a founding member of the New York State Council on the Arts.[12] Dance was his first love, and he believed that the National Museum of Dance and Hall of Fame had the potential to help make Saratoga Springs and the region a world center for dance.[13] The Lewis A. Swyer Company oversaw the renovation and reconstruction of the Washington Baths for the Museum, designed

FACING PAGE:
The foyer prior to the bathhouse reconstruction for the Museum, circa 1985.

TOP:
Water-damaged ceiling of the foyer prior to reconstruction, circa 1985.

BOTTOM:
Original mineral water fountain in the foyer.

by Saratoga Associates, with Swyer himself the driving force behind its completion for the 1986 preview season. Sharing the singular spirit they had together created in the Museum, he wrote to Marylou Whitney the following year, "I want you to know how very grateful I am for your interest that never flags and always brings its own very special brand of excitement and stardust, enhancing our efforts to make this a truly outstanding museum and dance center."[14]

The Washington Baths, a National Historic Landmark, is a wood-frame, single-story structure comprised of concrete and stucco panel with half-timber work and a patterned slate roof. Its architectural design is an amalgam of the arts and crafts (bungalow), Tudor, and neoclassical styles. Concrete columns with wood pergolas, and semicircular terraces stand on the exterior of each of the two wings of this highly distinct H-shaped building that totals nearly 33,000 square feet. A larger third terrace stands at the back of the structure, directly behind the foyer.

Between the time of the Washington Baths' closing in 1978 and its repurposing for the Museum in 1986, the building had fallen into complete disrepair. The initial phase of restoration and reconstruction of the Washington Baths included exterior repair and landscaping, and extensive interior repair due to water damage. Original bath fixtures were removed and some retained for projected future display. Insulation and climate control were installed, and scores of windows were replaced.

TOP LEFT AND RIGHT, BOTTOM:
Reconstruction and restoration of the bathhouse began in the mid-1980s.
FACING PAGE LEFT TO RIGHT:
Interior restoration, 1987.
Employee entrance prior to exterior renovation, 1985.

The Beaux Arts foyer was restored to its 1920s splendor. Its terrazzo floor was maintained, along with a mineral water fountain, no longer in use.[15] Wicker furniture original to the bathhouse was restored and repurposed. This elegant space was further enhanced with brass and crystal chandeliers given as a gift to the Museum by Mrs. Whitney. Two 5,000 square foot galleries flanking the foyer were constructed. Designed by Marty Bronson, gallery director at the Fashion Institute of Technology (FIT), the gallery walls were painted charcoal grey, intended to create an atmosphere of drama found in theaters.[16] In 1988, the Preservation League of New York State honored the National Museum of Dance and the Lewis A. Swyer Company with the Adaptive Use Award for the exemplary preservation and reuse of the historic Washington Baths. Today, this wonderfully unique building is a highly coveted venue for weddings and other special events, representing a significant portion of the Museum's annual income. The Museum provides use of its space free of charge to several not-for-profit organizations for fundraising events each year.

Athena, located in the front circle, is an iconic representation of the many forms of dance celebrated by the Museum.[17] This seven-foot-tall, scrap metal steel sculpture, created by the renowned American artist Judith Brown, was donated by Swyer's widow, Anne, in 1990. Brown's work is held in the permanent collections of the Museum of Modern Art and the Brooklyn Museum, and was largely inspired by classical sculpture and dance, especially the movement of Martha Graham.[18] An exhibition of her work, *Figures in Motion,* was presented at the Museum in 1989. Brown's *Athena* is the model from which sculptor Alice Manzi has created the current Hall of Fame awards since 2015.

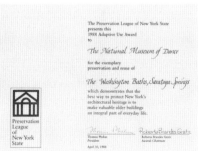

FACING PAGE:
The Museum foyer today.

TOP:
The front entrance of the Museum today with Judith Brown's *Athena* in the foreground.

BOTTOM:
The Preservation League of New York State 1988 Adaptive Use Award was given to the National Museum of Dance and the Lewis A. Swyer Company for the preservation and reuse of the Washington Baths.

THE WEEKEND PREMIERED with style and grace in Midtown Manhattan on the fifth of June, as 15 antique carriages stopped traffic along their 3 mile route at the noon hour.

An Evening in Old Saratoga

Media coverage of the founding of the Museum began immediately upon its announcement in 1984. By opening day, it had become national in scope, with articles from the *Boston Globe* to the *New York Times* to the *Los Angeles Times*. Marylou Whitney believed it was critical to introduce and develop the Museum beyond the confines of Saratoga Springs and the region. In doing so, on Thursday, June 5, 1986, Mrs. Whitney served as grand marshal of a Grand Carriage Parade in Manhattan. Fifteen antique horse-drawn carriages processed through Central Park and down Fifth Avenue to the Seagram Building at Park Avenue and 52nd Street, where participants including Saratoga Springs mayor Ellsworth Jones and art world luminaries such as Kitty Carlisle Hart, Andy

FACING PAGE:

The June 5, 1986 Grand Carriage Parade in Manhattan was organized to introduce *A Weekend in Old Saratoga* which included a fundraising gala to benefit the Museum during its preview season.

TOP LEFT TO RIGHT:

Judy Rosato, Mrs. Ellsworth Jones, Mayor of Saratoga Springs Ellsworth Jones, and Hornsman Charles Moll.

Actor Tony Randall and artist Andy Warhol at the champagne reception held mid-route at the Seagram Building.

BOTTOM, LEFT TO RIGHT:

Whip Dinwiddie Lampton Jr., Gala Chairman Dianne Knapp, Pamela Stokes, Georgiana Ducas, Whip George A. "Frolic" Weymouth, Kitty Carlisle Hart, and Grand Marshal Marylou Whitney in front of the Seagram Building on Park Avenue.

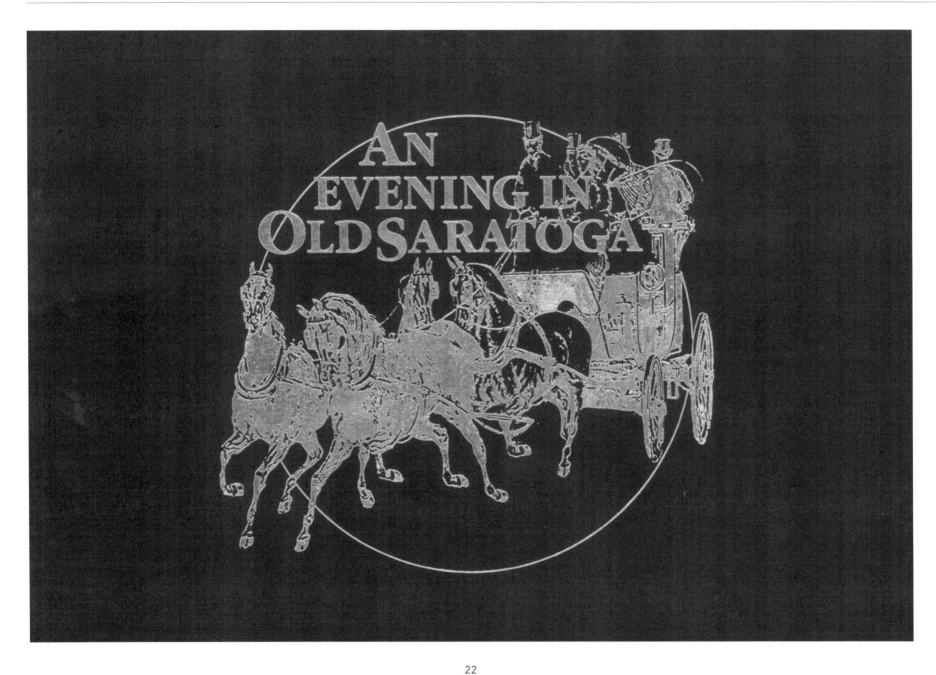

Warhol, Tony Randall, Peter Martins, and Cab Calloway stopped off for a champagne reception mid-route.[19] The parade, sponsored by Seagram's and the Concord Watch Company, continued up Madison Avenue to Central Park West, culminating at Tavern on the Green. The event was organized to promote *A Weekend in Old Saratoga*, which included *Great Western Champagne's An Evening in Old Saratoga*, an August 2 benefit in Saratoga Springs for the Museum. The unveiling of the new Concord Saratoga watch collection, still in production today, was reserved for the occasion. Attended by some five hundred guests including members of NYCB and celebrities such as Ginger Rogers and Walter Cronkite, it raised more than $40,000 for the Museum and inaugurated its legendary annual gala.[20]

FACING PAGE:
The program for *Great Western Champagne's An Evening in Old Saratoga* benefit for the Museum, August 2, 1986. Gift of the Swyer Family.

LEFT:
Museum founder Lewis A. Swyer and the Museum's first director, Alison Moore, at the 1986 gala.

RIGHT:
Marylou Whitney at the 1986 gala.

Preview Season

FACING PAGE:

Dressing the Ballet: Costumes from America's Most Celebrated Companies featured more than fifty costumes and was the first exhibition curated by the Museum in its 1986 preview season.

TOP AND BOTTOM:

The 1986 exhibition *Dressing the Ballet: Costumes from America's Most Celebrated Companies* was organized by costume designer and dance historian Malcolm McCormick and designed by Marty Bronson, gallery director at FIT.

In January 1986, as Phase One of the reconstruction was well underway, the Museum hired its first director. Alison Moore was an arts administrator for the State University of New York with discrete experience in the organization of exhibitions and dance festivals. With only part of the Washington Baths restored, the Museum presented a preview season from July 8 to September 30, 1986, that offered four exhibitions and a slate of programming. The Museum welcomed more than six thousand visitors in this three-month span.[21] *Dressing the Ballet: Costumes from America's Most Celebrated Ballet Companies* was the Museum's first curated exhibition. Organized by costume designer and dance historian, Malcolm McCormick, it featured more than fifty costumes from prominent companies such as American Ballet Theatre, Dance Theatre of Harlem, NYCB, Joffrey Ballet, Pacific Northwest Ballet, and San Francisco Ballet. *Made in America: Modern Dance Then and Now*, curated by dance historian Suzanne Shelton, was the American Dance Festival's fiftieth anniversary traveling photographic exhibition that chronicled the development of American modern dance from 1890 through the present day in one hundred eighty images. *Tracking, Tracing, Marking, Pacing* was organized by Ellen Schwartz, Pratt Institute, and the Dance Notation Bureau, and illustrated how choreographers visualize their three-dimensional, kinetic art form on a two-dimensional piece of paper.

This traveling exhibition featured works of art by Laura Dean, Lucinda Childs, and Oskar Schlemmer, among numerous others. *The National Museum of Dance: Development of a Dream*, installed in the foyer, was an introduction to the Museum using photos of the Washington Baths before and after reconstruction and plans for the completed project, including a highly detailed, 1″ = 8′ scale model of the proposed structure created by miniaturist Jack Van Dusen.[22] Marty Bronson from FIT designed and installed each of the preview season exhibitions.

Innovative, collaborative programming has remained a hallmark of the Museum for the past thirty years. The preview season established this standard with the Museum's sponsorship of a series of master classes coordinated with Skidmore College and SPAC featuring Laura Dean, the Alwin Nikolais Dance Theatre, and Hubbard Street Dance. The vast range of programming offered by the Museum has included lectures; book signings; group trips to concert dance performances;

pre-performance backstage tours for children at SPAC; symposiums; dance performances; concerts; dancer health, multicultural, and national dance days; film screenings; and a dynamic roster of master classes led by dancers and choreographers representing the full range of the art form.

The robust, extraordinary team of volunteers at the Museum was formed in advance of the 1986 preview season and was integral to all aspects of the Museum's function from readying the building for its July 8 opening to conducting tours and nearly everything in between. So strong was the belief in and commitment to the Museum at its inception that by the end of the 1987 season the volunteers for this small cultural institution totaled seventy individuals with some two thousand hours of donated service in all.[23]

RIGHT:
The American Dance Festival's fiftieth anniversary traveling photographic exhibition, *Made in America: Modern Dance Then and Now*, was presented during the Museum's 1986 preview season.

FACING PAGE:
Long-standing volunteers and the Museum's first director at the twenty-fifth anniversary celebration in 2011, from left, Kathleen Livesey, Anne Sherman, Maryanne Malecki, Diane Marchand, Margaret Chretian, Museum Director Alison Moore, Irma Mahar, Susan Edwards, Mary Anne Fantauzzi, Sharon Walsh, and Noreen Baker.

ARTHUR MURRAY FAVORITES

Capitol RECORDS

HIGH FIDELITY RECORDING

FRANCIS SCOTT
and his
orchestra

WALTZES

personally
recommended
for dancing
by
Arthur Murray

of Ballroom Dancing)

ARTHUR
MURRAY
FAVORITES

Capitol RECORDS

HIGH FIDELITY RECORDING

sambas

Capitol

RECORDS

Capitol

ARTHUR MURRAY FAVORITES——TANGOS
LES BAXTER AND HIS ORCHESTRA

EBF-263

PART 3
(F3-263)

1. JALOUSIE
(Jacob Gade)
2. EL CHOCLO
(A. G. Villoldo-Rachel)

Forty Five

CAPITOL RECORDS, INC. • HOLLYWOOD, CALIFOR

Arthur Murray's
LIBRARY OF
DANCE MUSIC

69¢ OR

FREE
with purch
INSTRU
RECORD

INTRODUCING
the
Twist

Arthur Murray Vinyl Records
Sambas (Donated by Lisa Kosek),
Leslie LaGuardia)
Arthur Murray Trophy (Donated by Leslie LaG
Arthur Murray released many music
could practice at home. T
was a key co

Tangos, The Twist (Dona

CHAPTER TWO

Exhibitions and Hall of Fame

The National Museum of Dance has mounted more than one hundred exhibitions over the course of its thirty-year history, by which it has sought to explore and present the tremendous scope of the art form. Through its annual exhibition schedule, Hall of Fame inductions, and special events, the Museum has collaborated with and hosted a vast range of choreographers, dancers, scholars, artists, designers, and artistic directors. The continued involvement, support, and interest of the dance community at large has inspired the Museum to further interpret and develop its mission.

FACING PAGE:
Display of Arthur Murray memorabilia and vinyl records in the Hall of Fame.

EXHIBITIONS AND HALL OF FAME

Within nine gallery spaces there are four permanent installations, the Art in the Foyer series, and a range of annually rotating exhibitions, including two each season that showcase the newest Hall of Fame inductees. The permanent installations include the Mr. and Mrs. Cornelius Vanderbilt Whitney Hall of Fame; the Alfred Z. Solomon Children's Wing, an interactive play space and gallery for children's artwork; *Washington Bathhouse*, a display of two adjoining, restored bath and treatment rooms containing original fixtures, equipment, and furniture that illustrate the history of the baths and the Museum building; and *Dancers in Film*, an exhibition that celebrates the synthesis and history of these art forms.

TOP:
The Alfred Z. Solomon Children's Wing.

BOTTOM LEFT AND RIGHT:
Views of a fully restored treatment room in the *Washington Bathhouse* permanent installation.

FACING PAGE:
The 1978 portrait of Mr. and Mrs. Cornelius Vanderbilt Whitney by celebrated Spanish-born artist Alejo Vidal-Quadras hangs at the entrance to the Hall of Fame.

MR. & MRS. CORNELIUS VANDERBILT WHITNEY
HALL OF FAME

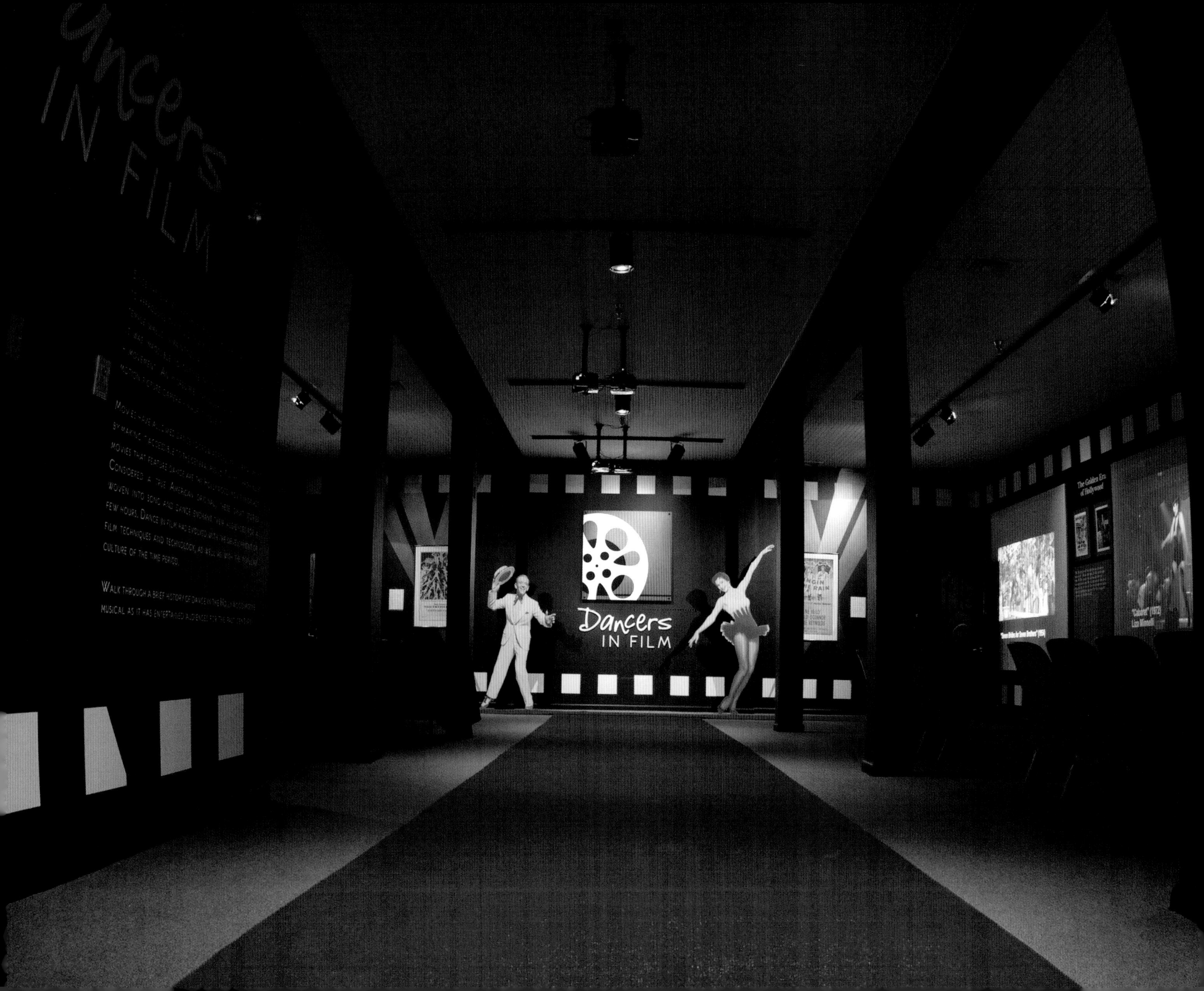
Dancers
IN FILM

Outdoor installations continue to be part of the Museum's exhibition programming and have included works by Judith Brown, Bogusław Lustyk, and Andrew DeVries. Most recently, sculptor Alice Manzi displayed her nine-piece work *Gen,* inspired by Gen Horiuchi's performance in Peter Martins's *Les Gentilhommes*. In 2013, board president Michele Riggi initiated the citywide art exhibition *Saratoga En Pointe,* to benefit the Museum and highlight Saratoga Springs as a cultural destination. More than thirty five-foot-tall pointe shoe sculptures were commissioned by local patrons and painted by local artists. After a one-time viewing at the Museum, they were placed throughout the city, where many remain in place. This program was created in conjunction with *En Pointe!,* a comprehensive exhibition co-curated by Leslie Roy-Heck, a former NYCB soloist, that explored the history, construction, myth, and truth of pointe shoes.[1]

FACING PAGE:
Dancers in Film, one of the Museum's permanent exhibitions, opened in 2014.

CLOCKWISE FROM TOP:
Sculptor Alice Manzi's nine-piece work *Gen* was installed on the front lawn of the Museum in 2016.

Pointe shoes on display at the Museum for a one-time viewing.

Ron and Michele Riggi at the Museum's opening reception for the city-wide art exhibition *Saratoga En Pointe* and the reopening of the newly renovated Hall of Fame, May 31, 2013.

The 2012 exhibition *En Pointe!* examined the history of pointe shoes.

The 1987 grand opening season exhibitions set the standard by which the Museum planned to develop into a nationally recognized cultural institution. In addition to *Shaping the American Dance Dream: The Founders*, the new permanent exhibition honoring the first thirteen Hall of Fame inductees, two other exhibitions were presented. The enormously popular *Shall We Dance? Costumes from Broadway and Hollywood,* was curated by veteran dancers, directors, and choreographers Rudy Tronto and Bill Bradley, and featured some forty costumes from stage and film. Garments such as Cecil Beaton–designed costumes from *My Fair Lady*, Ann Miller's and Mickey Rooney's costumes from the finale of *Sugar Babies*, Robert Preston's band uniform from the film *The Music Man*, a Rita Moreno–worn costume from the film *West Side Story*, and the tenth Gypsy Robe were included.[2] *Portraiture in Dance: Photographs by Kenn Duncan* was the first retrospective of the renowned photographer's work since his death the year before. Images of Twyla Tharp, Mikhail Baryshnikov, Judith Jamison, Natalia Makarova, and Gregory Hines were among those displayed. The Museum again presented Duncan's work in the 2009 exhibition *Red Shoes*, based on his 1984 book of the same name.

RIGHT:
Shaping the American Dance Dream: The Founders was mounted in the 1987 grand opening season and honored the first thirteen Hall of Fame inductees.

FACING PAGE LEFT AND RIGHT:
The 1987 exhibition *Shall We Dance? Costumes from Broadway and Hollywood* featured forty notable costumes including examples worn by Shirley Jones and Robert Preston in the 1962 film *The Music Man*.

35

Art in the Foyer

Since the 1986 preview season, the Museum's foyer has been utilized as a formal exhibition space for installations such as photographer David Michalek's *Visions of Dance* and *Spaces of the Mind: Isamu Noguchi's Dance Designs*, a photography exhibition curated by dance scholar Robert Tracy in conjunction with the publication of his book that shared this title. Black and white images documenting Noguchi's work mainly for the Martha Graham Dance Company and NYCB by a host of eminent photographers such as Arnold Eagle and Philippe Halsman were displayed.[3] In 2006, this concept was defined and formalized as Art in the Foyer, a rotating series of dance-related fine art.[4] In its beginning years, Art in the Foyer featured several installations in a single season; photographer Lawrence White was the first to exhibit within this program.

FACING PAGE:
Lawrence White photograph of dancer Nanna Andersen taken on the Staten Island Ferry, circa 2000. This photograph was displayed in White's 2002 exhibition *The Art of Light–The Art of Dance*.

LEFT:
Isamu Noguchi designed the set as well as Martha Graham's headdress, cuffs, and collar for Graham's 1950 dance work *Judith*.

FACING PAGE:
Malcolm McCormick costume designs for Zachary Solov's *Invitation to the Dance*, performed by Ballet Souffle. Loie Fuller Butterfly costume. Queen Bee costume. Gift of Malcolm McCormick.

CLOCKWISE FROM TOP LEFT:
Paul Kolnik photographs of the Broadway revival of *A Chorus Line* (2006–2008), direction by Bob Avian, choreography reconstruction by Baayork Lee. Based on the original Broadway production conceived, choreographed, and directed by Michael Bennett, with Bob Avian, co-choreographer.

Board member Carol Swyer and photographer Paul Kolnik at the opening of his 2016 Art in the Foyer exhibition, *Moment to Moment: A History of Time and Place*.

Students from the Museum's School of the Arts at the opening reception for *Moment to Moment: A History of Time and Place*, May 6, 2016.

It now features a single artist's work for an entire year. Although the medium most featured has been photography, others have been presented, including the costume sketches of designer and dance historian Malcolm McCormick in the thirtieth anniversary season in 2017. In recent years, some of the country's most celebrated dance photographers have been highlighted in Art in the Foyer. Lois Greenfield presented her series *Celestial Bodies/Infernal Souls* in 2010. The following year, Rose Eichenbaum's exhibitions *Masters of Movement* and *From the Wings* were on view. In 2012, the Museum displayed a collection of Christopher Duggan's photographs from the Jacob's Pillow Inside/Out series, and in 2013 Jordan Matter exhibited, for the first time, photographs from his acclaimed book *Dancers Among Us: A Celebration of Joy in the Everyday*. Paul Kolnik, renowned photographer of NYCB, Alvin Ailey American Dance Theater, and Broadway, has held two exhibitions in the foyer, *Broadway, Ballet, and Beyond,* and *Moment to Moment: A History of Time and Place*, and has contributed work to various other exhibitions at the Museum.[5]

TOP:
Jordan Matter signing copies of his book *Dancers Among Us: A Celebration of Joy in the Everyday* at the 2013 opening of his Art in the Foyer exhibition.

BOTTOM:
Lois Greenfield's 2010 Art in the Foyer exhibition *Celestial Bodies/Infernal Souls*.

FACING PAGE:
Jordan Matter and dancers from the Museum's School of the Arts at his 2013 exhibition opening.

Ballet for a City and a Nation: Forty Years of the New York City Ballet

The first exhibition at the Museum to highlight NYCB, *Ballet for a City and a Nation,* was curated by dance scholar Susan Au, together with founding board member and president of Ballet Society Nancy Norman Lassalle and Edward Bigelow, veteran NYCB dancer and company manager. Lassalle was involved with five NYCB exhibitions in total at the Museum, with Bigelow a collaborator on three of them.[6] *Ballet for a City and a Nation* celebrated the fortieth anniversary of NYCB in 1988 through an extensive installation that included some thirty costumes designed by luminaries such as Barbara Karinska, Cecil Beaton, and Santo Loquasto; Rouben Ter-Arutunian's original 1964 set designs for *George Balanchine's The Nutcracker®*; international tour posters for performances in Russia, France, Israel, Japan, and beyond from the 1950s and 60s; and numerous photographs.

FACING PAGE:
Children's costumes from *Don Quixote* (1965), choreography by George Balanchine, masks and armor designed by Lawrence Vlady, as displayed in the 1988 exhibition *Ballet for a City and a Nation: Forty Years of the New York City Ballet.* ©The George Balanchine Trust. Gift of NYCB.

LEFT:
Sallie Wilson posing with the costume she wore as Queen Elizabeth I in the first section of *Episodes* (1959), choreography by George Balanchine and Martha Graham, costumes by Karinska. ©The George Balanchine Trust.

LEFT TO RIGHT:
Costume from *Pulcinella* (1972), choreography by George Balanchine and Jerome Robbins, costumes by Eugene Berman and masks by Kermit Love. ©The George Balanchine Trust.

Poster for the September 20, 1956 NYCB performance at the Venice Biennale's Nineteenth Festival of Contemporary Music. Gift of NYCB.

Costumes from *The Steadfast Tin Soldier* (1975) which had its world premiere at SPAC, choreography by George Balanchine, costumes by David Mitchell. ©The George Balanchine Trust.

FACING PAGE LEFT:
Costumes worn by Gelsey Kirkland as the Nightingale and Elise Flagg as the Mechanical Bird in *The Song of the Nightingale* (1972), choreography by John Taras, costumes by Rouben Ter-Arutunian.

FACING PAGE RIGHT TOP AND BOTTOM:
Tour posters from NYCB performances from June 29 to July 3 at the Stadsschouwburg Theater in Amsterdam as part of the 1955 Holland Festival. Gift of NYCB.

HOLLAND FESTIVAL 1955

STADSSCHOUWBURG

NEW YORK CITY BALLET

Artistic Director GEORGE BALANCHINE

Associate Artistic Director JEROME ROBBINS

MARIA TALLCHIEF	TANAQUIL LECLERQ	DIANA ADAMS
PATRICIA WILDE	MELISSA HAYDEN	JILLANA
NICHOLAS MAGALLANES	FRANCISCO MONCION	HERBERT BLISS
TODD BOLENDER	ROY TOBIAS	JACQUES D'AMBOISE

CAROLYN GEORGE   BARBARA WALCZAK   BARBARA FALLIS   BARBARA MILBERG

and

ANDRÉ EGLEVSKY

LE GRAND CORPS DE BALLET

HET ROTTERDAMSCH PHILHARMONISCH ORKEST

Musical Director	General Director	Technical Director
LEON BARZIN	**LINCOLN KIRSTEIN**	**JEAN ROSENTHAL**

Woensdag 29 Juni, 8 uur **GALA VOORSTELLING**	Serenade · La Valse · Sylvia Pas de deux Western Symphony
Donderdag 30 Juni, 8 uur	Lac des Cygnes · Four Temperaments Apres-Midi d'un Faune · Symphony in C
Vrijdag 1 Juli, 8 uur	Serenade · Scotch Symphony · Pas de trois Pied Piper
Zaterdag 2 Juli, 8 uur	The Duel · Scotch Symphony · The Cage Pied Piper
Zondag 3 Juli, 8 uur	Lac des Cygnes · The Cage · Pas de trois Western Symphony

European Tour under the exclusive Management of
L. LEONIDOFF
45, RUE LA BOÉTIE, PARIS 8

Plaatsen van f 2.— tot f 20.— van Woensdag 8 Juni af dagelijks van 10—3 uur aan
de kassa van de Stadsschouwburg verkrijgbaar.   N.V. Van Munster's Drukkerijen · Amsterdam

Firebird and the New York City Ballet 1949–1995

Co-curated by Nancy Norman Lassalle and Edward Bigelow in 1995, *Firebird and the New York City Ballet 1949-1995* was considered a landmark exhibition at the Museum. Through original sketches, costumes, photographs, posters, playbills, memorabilia, scenery, and props, this exhibition traced the history of the ballet back to its earliest performance by Serge Diaghilev's Ballets Russes in 1910, who first commissioned the score from Igor Stravinsky, forward to the 1970 NYCB recension of *Firebird,* and ultimately to the present day.[7] The show highlighted the collaboration between Stravinsky, George Balanchine, Jerome Robbins, Marc Chagall, and Barbara Karinska, and explored the various executions of the original Chagall costume designs and the subtle changes in choreography over these years. Maria Tallchief, the first Firebird in 1949, attended the exhibition opening, as did former principal dancer Karin von Aroldingen who performed the role throughout the 1970s. Marc Chagall's granddaughter Bella Meyer also attended the opening reception and the performance of *Firebird* at SPAC that followed.[8]

FACING PAGE:
Headpiece from *Firebird* (1949), choreography by George Balanchine and Jerome Robbins, costumes designed by Marc Chagall and executed by Karinska. ©The George Balanchine Trust. Gift of NYCB.

LEFT:
Francisco Moncion and Maria Tallchief were in the original cast of *Firebird* (1949), choreography by George Balanchine and Jerome Robbins, costumes designed by Marc Chagall and executed by Karinska. ©The George Balanchine Trust.

FACING PAGE, LEFT TOP AND BOTTOM:
Marc Chagall sets and costumes from
Firebird (1949), choreography by George
Balanchine and Jerome Robbins. ©The
George Balanchine Trust.

FACING PAGE, RIGHT:
Maria Tallchief, NYCB's first *Firebird*, attended
the exhibition opening on July 20, 1995.

LEFT:
Costumes from *Firebird* (1949),
choreography by George Balanchine and
Jerome Robbins, costumes designed by
Marc Chagall and executed by Karinska.
©The George Balanchine Trust.

RIGHT:
NYCB's Karin von Aroldingen, who
performed the role of the *Firebird*
throughout the 1970s, attended the
exhibition opening.

Les Ballets 1933

Traveling exhibitions have represented an important aspect of the Museum's schedule, especially in its infancy, for both broader content and exposure. One such example was the loan of *Les Ballets 1933* from The Royal Pavilion Art Gallery and Museums in Brighton, England, curated by Jane Pritchard. Through original designs, costumes, props, and photographs, the history of the short-lived troupe was revealed and contextualized. Les Ballets 1933 was George Balanchine's first company in the West, founded together with the poet and librettist Boris Kochno, and sponsored by Edward James whose collection this display drew from. Collaborators of Les Ballets 1933 were among the most avant-garde of the time: Christian Bérard, André Derain, Pavel Tchelitchew, Darius Milhaud, Kurt Weill, Bertolt Brecht, and Barbara Karinska. Dancers included Tamara Toumanova, Tilly Losch, Diana Gould, and Kyra Blanc. It was solely because of the artistry of Les Ballets 1933 that Balanchine was first invited by Lincoln Kirstein to establish himself and his career in the United States, a pivotal moment in the history of American ballet.

FACING PAGE:
Future artistic collaborators of Les Ballets 1933 on stage in Monte Carlo after a performance of George Balanchine's *Cotillon* (1932) for Colonel de Basil's Ballets Russes, from left: designer Christian Bérard, librettist Boris Kochno, choreographer René Blum, de Basil, répétiteur Sergei Grigoriev, and Balanchine, 1932. BALANCHINE is a Trademark of The George Balanchine Trust.

ABOVE:
Cover of the Museum catalog for *Les Ballets 1933* containing a costume sketch by Pavel Tchelitchew for *L'Errante* (1933).

The Museum enhanced the installation with artifacts from additional sources such as the Jerome Robbins Dance Division of the New York Public Library for the Performing Arts. Anna Kisselgoff described the exhibition as "trailblazing" in the *New York Times*.[9] It traveled on to the New York Public Library at Lincoln Center and was the exhibition for which the Museum produced its first catalog.[10]

LEFT TO RIGHT:
Pavel Tchelitchew, self-portrait, 1933.

German composer Kurt Weill backstage at the Théâtre des Champs-Élysées, 1933.

Tilly Losch as the Nun and Léonide Massine as the Spielman in Massine's revival of *The Miracle* for C. B. Cochran in London, 1932.

FACING PAGE, LEFT TO RIGHT:
Kyra Blanc and Karl Scheibe in *Les Songes* (1933), choreography by George Balanchine, costumes by André Derain. ©The George Balanchine Trust.

Tilly Losch in *L'Errante* (1933), choreography by George Balanchine, costumes by Pavel Tchelitchew. ©The George Balanchine Trust.

100 Years of Russian Ballet: 1830–1930

Another significant traveling exhibition at the Museum in 1990 was *100 Years of Russian Ballet: 1830–1930*, a monumental and unprecedented loan from the collection of the Leningrad State Museum of Theater and Music. Some four hundred works of art, never before seen in the United States, comprised this exhibition that documented the golden age of Russian ballet and served as a vital cultural exchange at the end of the Cold War. The spokesperson for *100 Years of Russian Ballet* was ballerina and actress Tamara Geva, the first wife of George Balanchine and the daughter of the founder of the Leningrad State Museum of Theater and Music. It was curated by an international team of dance scholars and first displayed at Eduard Nakhamkin Fine Arts in Manhattan before traveling to Saratoga Springs. Highlights of the installation included personal objects from Igor Stravinsky and Anna Pavlova, Tamara Karsavina's ballet slippers, original costumes from the 1890 premiere of *The Sleeping Beauty*, and scenery and costume designs by Léon Bakst among numerous others. Also included were several Serge Diaghilev-era sets loaned by prima ballerina Natalia Makarova.

FACING PAGE:
Headpiece displayed in the 1990 exhibition
100 Years of Russian Ballet: 1830–1930.

LEFT:
Guests from Leningrad at the opening
reception for *100 Years of Russian Ballet:
1830–1930*, May 1990.

The monumental exhibition *100 Years of Russian Ballet: 1830-1930* featured some four hundred works of art, including dozens of costumes, that had never before been displayed in the United States. This unprecedented loan from the Leningrad State Museum of Theater and Music represented a vital culture exchange at the end of the Cold War.

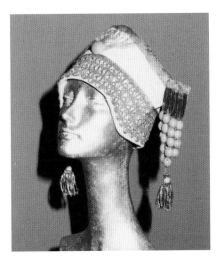

Jean Erdman: Masks, Costumes and Stagecraft from her World of Dance and Myth

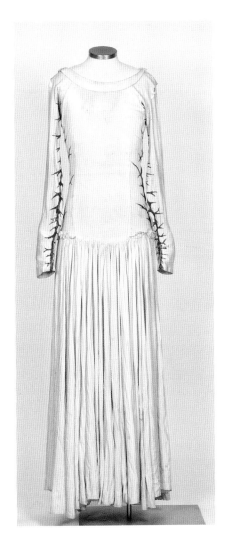

The 1998 season celebrated three pioneers of modern dance in exhibition programming—Jean Erdman, Anna Sokolow, and José Limón.[11] Erdman was honored with a substantial exhibition, *Jean Erdman: Masks, Costumes and Stagecraft from her World of Dance and Myth*. Curated by Nancy Allison, artistic director of Jean Erdman Dance, this installation incorporated original costumes, dynamic scores, designs, photographs, and masks to illustrate and examine her singular perspective, choreography, and aesthetic. Vital collaborations with her husband, the mythologist Joseph Campbell, and others such as John Cage, Lou Harrison, e.e. cummings, and Maya Deren were articulated. Masks created for Erdman's dance works by Ralph Lee, former Erdman dancer and artistic director of the Mettawee River Theatre Company, were featured throughout the exhibition. Jean Erdman attended the opening and Nancy Allison led an open master class in Erdman technique and choreography. At the close of the exhibition, costumes from seminal Erdman works including *Ophelia* and *The Coach with the Six Insides* were donated to the Museum as part of the permanent collection.

FACING PAGE:
Jean Erdman with Nancy Allison at the opening reception for *Jean Erdman: Masks, Costumes, and Stagecraft from her World of Dance and Myth*, May 27, 1998.

CLOCKWISE FROM LEFT:
Costume worn by Jean Erdman in her seminal work *Ophelia* (1946). Erdman choreographed this solo to a commissioned score by John Cage; the costume was designed by his wife, Xenia Cage. Gift of Jean Erdman Dance.

Headpiece worn by Erdman in her celebrated dance drama *The Coach with the Six Insides* (1962), based on James Joyce's *Finnegans Wake*. Erdman's costume was designed by Gail Ito. Gift of Jean Erdman Dance.

Erdman performing in *The Coach with the Six Insides* (1962). Gift of Jean Erdman Dance.

JACK MITCHELL
NYC

62

Classic Black

The Museum has utilized the unparalleled collection at the Jerome Robbins Dance Division of the New York Public Library for the Performing Arts for loans, research, and curatorial collaboration for the past thirty years.[12] *Classic Black*, an exhibition organized by the Dance Division from an oral history project conducted there, was presented at the Museum in 2002. Through photographs from the Library and costumes supplemented by the Museum from Alvin Ailey American Dance Theater, NYCB, and American Ballet Theatre, *Classic Black* conveyed the history of African American ballet dancers in this country and the innovative teachers and choreographers who created a niche for these dancers in the world of classical ballet between 1930 and 1970. Dancers highlighted included mavericks such as Raven Wilkinson, Arthur Mitchell, Talley Beatty, Judith Jamison, Louis Johnson, and Doris Jones. Veteran dancers Virginia Johnson, Delores Brown Abelson, and Walter Nicks comprised a panel for discussion at the exhibition opening, led by the exhibition's curator, Madeleine Nichols.

FACING PAGE:
Nat Horne, Charles Queenan, and Charles Moore in *Gotham Suite* (1954), choreography by Tony Charmoli, Negro Dance Theatre.

LEFT:
Doris Jones, founder of the Jones-Haywood Dance School in Washington, D.C., with students.

FACING PAGE, LEFT:
Janet Collins was the first African American prima ballerina at the Metropolitan Opera.

FACING PAGE, RIGHT:
Bernard Johnson in *Gotham Suite* (1954), choreography by Tony Charmoli, Negro Dance Theatre.

ABOVE:
Italian Concerto (1954–55) choreography by Aubrey Hitchins, Negro Dance Theatre.

Dancing Rebels: The New Dance Group

It is believed that all modern dancers in this country can trace their artistic lineage back to the New Dance Group, a revolutionary community of young dancers, choreographers, and teachers committed to upholding social justice through their work.[13] Founded in 1932 in New York City, the New Dance Group taught scores of students of all races, religions, and financial circumstance, and provided a place where dancers could make and perform new work, among them artists such as Donald McKayle, Pearl Primus, Hadassah, Eve Gentry, Sophie Maslow, and Daniel Nagrin. This watershed exhibition was curated in 2005 by Carolyn Adams and Julie Adams Strandberg, founders of the American Dance Legacy Initiative and students of the New Dance Group. It conveyed the abundant history of the collective from the 1930s to the 1950s through costumes, soundscapes, set pieces, programs, posters, and performance video culled from original members and dance companies across the country.

FACING PAGE:

The 2005 exhibition *Dancing Rebels: The New Dance Group*, curated by Carolyn Adams and Julie Adams Standberg, honored the abundant history of the New Dance Group from the 1930s to the 1950s.

LEFT:

The costumes for Sophie Maslow's seminal work *The Village I Knew* (1949), based on short stories by Sholem Aleichem, were designed by Eileen Holding.

The New Dance Group was inducted into the Hall of Fame the following year. Mary Anthony, Jean-Léon Destiné, Joseph Gifford, and Muriel Mannings, four of its earliest artists, attended the induction ceremony and accepted the award. *Dancing Rebels: The New Dance Group* inspired a robust schedule of programming that included an unprecedented five-day conference offering lecture demonstrations, master classes, workshops, panel discussions, and dance concerts.

FACING PAGE, CLOCKWISE FROM TOP LEFT:
Several costumes from *The Village I Knew* (1949), a dance work by Sophie Maslow that explored her Jewish roots, were on display in the 2005 exhibition *Dancing Rebels: The New Dance Group.*

LEFT:
Original members of the New Dance Group at the August 12, 2006, Hall of Fame induction, from left: Jean-Léon Destiné, Muriel Mannings, Joseph Gifford, and Mary Anthony.

RIGHT:
1953 performance poster for the New Dance Group.

125 Years of Tango: A Walk through the History of the Dance

The most recent in a series of exhibitions that have celebrated cultural dance forms, *125 Years of Tango: A Walk through the History of the Dance* was the first exhibition of its kind to chronicle the evolution of Argentine tango from the nineteenth century to the present day.[14] Drawn from the private collection of the show's curator, Antón Gazenbeek, it featured rare costumes, music, artifacts, and film footage, much of which was displayed publicly for the first time. Gazenbeek, internationally renowned tango dancer and historian, is understood to hold the largest tango archive in the world. *125 Years of Tango* explored the rich history of the dance form by decade and through themes such as music, dance styles, fashion, and the unique contributions of women. Gazenbeek and his husband, Jody Gazenbeek-Person, performed at the exhibition opening, demonstrating a range of tango styles from primitive to modern.

FACING PAGE:
The 2015 exhibition *125 Years of Tango: A Walk through the History of the Dance*.

LEFT:
Jody Gazenbeek-Person and exhibition curator, Antón Gazenbeek, performing at the opening reception on March 21, 2015.

Tango Performance Heels
Used on stage for 20 years in major tango shows by Anu Maria Rojas, New York City's pioneering tango Maestra.
~1986

FACING PAGE:

125 Years of Tango: A Walk through the History of the Dance, was comprised of the world-renowned tango collection of the show's curator, Antón Gazenbeek.

LEFT:

The Museum and School of the Arts mascot, Shrek, and installation associate, Tom Stone, inspecting the progress of *125 Years of Tango: A Walk through the History of the Dance.*

Super Bowl X Football
Signed by game MVP, Lynn Swann, 1976.

Courtesy of the Pro Football Hall of

Lynn Swann Signed
Ballet and Tap Shoes

The Dancing Athlete

One of the most innovative exhibitions curated by the Museum, *The Dancing Athlete*, examined the inherent connections between dance and sports, dancers and athletes, and artistry and athleticism, and this discrete dialogue that has been in place for centuries in the United States, Europe, and Russia. Themes such as sports-inspired choreography, shared movement vocabularies, and cross-training were explored across various dance forms and within ten sports that included skiing, basketball, hockey, soccer, skating, football, boxing, equestrian, baseball, and tennis. Special sections dedicated to the Olympics and

FACING PAGE:
Lynn Swann artifacts from *The Dancing Athlete*.

LEFT, TOP AND BOTTOM:
Artifacts in the baseball section of The Dancing Athlete included a Mika Piazza-signed baseball from the 2000 subway series, a gift of Michael Reilly, and a Mariano Rivera-signed glove, loaned by Ron and Michele Riggi.

The Dancer Athlete-Athlete Dancer section of the exhibition.

individuals who embody the roles of both dancer and athlete were also featured, including Edward Villella, Sugar Ray Robinson, Lynn Swann, and Misty Copeland. Costumes and uniforms, photographs, video, artifacts, and archival materials illustrated this deep nexus. *The Dancing Athlete* sparked a unique and robust programming schedule at the Museum that included sports-inspired dance classes and commissioned dance works for both the exhibition opening and the 2016 gala, *The Dancing Athlete*.[15]

LEFT AND RIGHT:
The Dancing Athlete examined the connection between artistry and athleticism within ten sports including skiing, basketball, hockey, soccer, skating, football, boxing, equestrian, baseball, and tennis.

FACING PAGE, LEFT:
The Flair, by Richard MacDonald, was created for the 1996 summer Olympic games in Atlanta. Gift of Michael Reilly.

FACING PAGE, RIGHT TOP AND BOTTOM:
1988 Olympian Bruce Bolesky and World Cup freestyle champion and Museum board member John Witt, both featured in the skiing section, at the opening reception, April 23, 2016.

The skiing section featured a Bogner ski suit worn by Suzy Chaffee in the film *Fire and Ice* (1986), loaned by the Vermont Ski and Snowboard Museum.

The Flair
Richard MacDonald, bronze, Art X inches.
This Flair, a three-set bronze sculpture of a gymnast,
was originally created for the 1996 Atlanta Olympics by
American artist Richard MacDonald.
Courtesy of Richard MacDonald

"Skiing moguls is like a dance...Gliding down the fall-line, turning with rhythm, turning left right and jumping is mogul skiing"

John Witt, World Cup freestyle champion

ABOVE AND LEFT:
The Old Ballgame, choreographed by
Joan K. Anderson and performed by
students from the Museum's
School of the Arts for *The Dancing Athlete*
gala on August 13, 2016.

RIGHT:
Brian Simerson choreographed and
performed a sports-inspired work,
Metamorphosis, for the April 23, 2016
opening of *The Dancing Athlete*.

FACING PAGE:
The Adirondack Thunder minor league
hockey team toured *The Dancing Athlete* as
part of the extensive programming schedule
for the exhibition.

Mr. and Mrs. Cornelius Vanderbilt Whitney Hall of Fame

Dedicated to Mr. and Mrs. Cornelius Vanderbilt Whitney in appreciation of their sponsorship and establishment of the Museum, the Hall of Fame honors innovators who have made an indelible contribution to American professional dance across all genres. As articulated by Lewis A. Swyer at its inauguration, "The Hall of Fame aims to illuminate the contributions of great choreographers, teachers, artistic directors, and others, living and dead, who have helped to shape and continue to shape American dance, in ballet, modern and contemporary dance, musical theater, and film."[16]

On June 2, 1987, the first thirteen inductees were revealed at Tiffany and Co. in Manhattan. Some two hundred guests attended the cocktail reception at which Fred Astaire, George Balanchine, Agnes de Mille, Isadora Duncan, Katherine Dunham, Martha Graham, Doris Humphrey, Lincoln Kirstein, Catherine Littlefield, Bill "Bojangles" Robinson, Ruth St. Denis, Ted Shawn, and Charles Weidman were announced as the founders of professional dance in America. Following the reception some thirty guests were invited to the Whitneys' Fifth Avenue penthouse for a Yugoslavian dinner.[17]

FACING PAGE:
Marylou Whitney with board members Roger Jakubowski and William E. Murray at the June 2, 1987 press reception at Tiffany and Co.

CLOCKWISE FROM TOP LEFT:
Marylou Whitney pays tribute to the first thirteen Hall of Fame inductees.

Nancy Norman Lassalle, John Taras, and Herb Chesbrough at the Tiffany and Co. reception.

Mrs. Whitney with Tiffany and Co. chairman William R. Chaney and Mrs. Chaney.

CLOCKWISE FROM TOP LEFT:
The first thirteen Hall of Fame awards in 1987 were created by glass artist Milon Townsend. Each one was a unique design for the recipient.

Bob Fosse's 2007 Hall of Fame award.

This stained glass Hall of Fame award was designed and made by the artist Hope Hawthorne from 1989 to 1998.

Gene Kelly's 2014 Hall of Fame award designed by Waterford Crystal.

Tommy Tune's 2009 Hall of Fame award designed by Waterford Crystal.

FACING PAGE:
The current Hall of Fame award is a bronze reproduction of Judith Brown's *Athena*, cast by the artist Alice Manzi.

The Hall of Fame honorees are chosen by a selection committee that has ranged in size and scope over the years. The first committee was comprised of Selma Jean Cohen, editor of the *International Encyclopedia of Dance*; Jack Haley Jr., award-winning Hollywood director, producer, and writer; Bella Lewitzky, pioneering modern dancer and choreographer; Harvey Lichtenstein, president of the Brooklyn Academy of Music; Arthur Mitchell, founder and director of Dance Theatre of Harlem; John Taras, associate director of American Ballet Theatre; and Liz Thompson, executive director of Jacob's Pillow Dance Festival. The Hall of Fame selection committee is currently comprised of a significant group of twenty-seven dance professionals including dancers, choreographers, scholars, teachers, and artistic directors representing an array of dance styles. The Hall of Fame selection process has remained intact over the course of thirty years with each member creating a list of potential candidates, and those with the most nominations are chosen as the inductees. Today, two inductees are chosen each year, one living and one deceased.

The Hall of Fame award itself has been recreated several times through the years. For the first class of inductees, glass artist Milon Townsend designed thirteen different awards, each one unique to the recipient. In 1988, Pierrepont T. Noyes, chairman of Oneida Ltd. and vice chairman of SPAC, designed a silver charger for inductees Busby Berkeley, Lucia Chase, Hanya Holm, John Martin, and Antony Tudor. Jerome Robbins was the sole inductee in 1989 and so began artist Hope Hawthorne's long tenure as the designer of the Hall of Fame award.[18] Inductees are now presented with a reproduction of the Museum's iconic sculpture *Athena*, cast by artist Alice Manzi.

Katherine Dunham was the first living inductee to accept her Hall of Fame award in person, stating in her remarks, "I'm very grateful for a building like this…for what it says."[19] For the dance professionals that have accepted their awards in person, this sentiment seems to have been largely universal—Merce Cunningham, Paul Taylor, Anna Sokolow, Arthur Mitchell, Fayard Nicholas, New Dance Group, Bill T. Jones, Peter Martins, Tommy Tune, Edward Villella, Suzanne Farrell, Marge Champion, Frankie Manning, Ben Vereen, Judith Jamison, Jacques d'Amboise, Mark Morris, and Patricia Wilde.[20] So too has this perspective been echoed by the prodigious group of individuals who have accepted the honor on behalf of deceased or infirm inductees.

CLOCKWISE FROM TOP LEFT:
Jane Sherman and Barton Mumaw who accepted the awards for Ruth St. Denis and Ted Shawn.

Katherine Dunham accepting her Hall of Fame award with her protégé Dr. Glory Van Scott looking on.

Marylou and Cornelius Vanderbilt Whitney and Lewis A. Swyer at the grand opening of the Hall of Fame, July 11, 1987.

FACING PAGE LEFT SIDE,
CLOCKWISE FROM TOP LEFT:
Anna Sokolow at her Hall of Fame induction, July 19, 1998.

Alvin Ailey's mother, Lula Cooper, at his Hall of Fame induction, June 11, 1992.

Merce Cunningham at his Hall of Fame induction, June 20, 1993.

Judith Jamison and Michele Riggi at Jamison's Hall of Fame induction at the Copacabana gala, August 10, 2013.

Fayard Nicholas and his wife Katherine at his Hall of Fame induction, August 5, 2001.

FACING PAGE, RIGHT TOP TO BOTTOM:
Savion Glover and Patricia Wilde at her Hall of Fame induction and that of Gregory Hines at The Dancing Athlete gala, August 13, 2016.

Jacques d'Amboise at his Hall of Fame meet and greet event, August 10, 2014.

The Hall of Fame induction ceremonies have furthered the Museum's mission of being a living museum. Often garnering hundreds of guests, live performance by some of the country's most celebrated dancers and companies has been a cornerstone of these events. The 2001 induction of Harold and Fayard Nicholas is counted among the most legendary, during which Savion Glover, at the culmination of his performance honoring the virtuosity and groundbreaking careers of the Nicholas Brothers, dropped to his knees in front of Fayard, in complete reverence for the tap master. Glover returned to the Museum in 2016 to accept the Hall of Fame induction of his mentor, Gregory Hines.

CLOCKWISE FROM TOP RIGHT:
Paul Taylor and dancers from Taylor 2 at his Hall of Fame induction, May 27, 1995.

Michele Riggi, Tommy Tune, and Gracey Tune performing at the *Gala on Broadway*, August 1, 2009, the night before his induction into the Hall of Fame.

Ben Vereen performing at his Hall of Fame induction at the *Song and Dance* gala, August 11, 2012.

FACING PAGE:
Jamar Roberts of Alvin Ailey American Dance Theater performing at Judith Jamison's Hall of Fame induction at the *Copacabana* gala, August 10, 2013.

The Museum's foyer has served as a monument to the Hall of Fame since 1987, when the names of the first thirteen inductees were placed along the frieze, a tradition that endures. The permanent Hall of Fame installation highlighting the individual achievements of each inductee has had four variants. Located in the Museum's north gallery, *Shaping the American Dance Dream: The Founders* was the first Hall of Fame exhibition, curated by Susan Au and designed by Marty Bronson and Associates with the close cooperation of Genevieve Oswald and the Dance Division of the New York Public Library. The Hall of Fame was redesigned in 1992 under the direction of Norton Owen, director of preservation at Jacob's Pillow, in collaboration with Kevan Moss Design and dance writer Mindy Aloff. Large-scale panels were created for each inductee with newly researched biographical information and documentary photographs. This installation was in place for fifteen years and expanded with new panels at each induction. In 2007, the Hall of Fame was relocated to the south gallery and reorganized by genre including modern, post-modern, ballet, Broadway, and contemporary dance, among others. This version included, for the first time, costumes and other three dimensional objects as part of the permanent installation, setting the stage for the next iteration of the Hall of Fame.

FACING PAGE:
The Hall of Fame was renovated in 1992 under the direction of Norton Owen in collaboration with Kevan Moss Design and dance writer Mindy Aloff.

LEFT TOP:
The names of Hall of Fame honorees grace the frieze in the Museum foyer.

LEFT BOTTOM:
The Hall of Fame, circa 1992.

CLOCKWISE FROM TOP LEFT:
In 2007, the Hall of Fame was redesigned and relocated to the south gallery.

FACING PAGE:
In 2013, the Hall of Fame was completely redesigned.

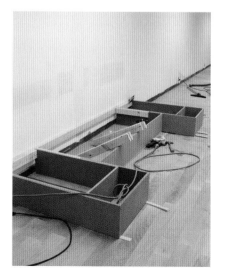

In 2013, Marylou Whitney and John Hendrickson sponsored the complete renovation and redesign of the Hall of Fame. The south gallery was divided into two exhibition spaces—one to house the permanent installation and one to house the annually rotating exhibitions honoring the current season's inductees. The new design for the vestibule included a five-foot circular inlaid marble floor medallion containing the logo, a crystal chandelier, and ionic columns, evocative of the Museum's Beaux Arts foyer and reflective of its long history. A portrait of Mr. and Mrs. Cornelius Vanderbilt Whitney by internationally-renowned, Spanish-born artist, Alejo Vidal-Quadras was installed at this entrance. New flooring was laid and display cases were built in the permanent installation to contain a plethora of significant costumes, artifacts, and works of fine art related to inductees that would now characterize the Hall of Fame. Small biographical plaques dedicated to each honoree replaced large text panels, allowing for a more visual experience. Highlights include costumes worn by Arthur Mitchell, Ruth St. Denis, Doris Humphrey, and Antony Tudor, and sculpture such as *The Village* (1960) by the Japanese artist Yasuhide Kobashi, commissioned by inductee Lincoln Kirstein. The new Hall of Fame reopened on May 31, 2013, at which Anna Pavlova was inducted as its forty-ninth member.

FACING PAGE, CLOCKWISE FROM TOP LEFT:
The Hall of Fame under construction and complete in 2013.

TOP:
The 2013 Hall of Fame redesign was underwritten by Marylou Whitney and John Hendrickson, pictured here with Michele Riggi at the reopening on May 31, 2013.

BOTTOM:
The Hall of Fame today.

Several large-scale exhibitions honoring individual inductees were created throughout the 1990s. Norton Owen and Kevan Moss together created six of the most compelling installations over the course of the decade, distinguished by their scholarship and innovative design. *Ted Shawn: A Centennial Tribute to the Father of American Dance,* in 1991, was their first collaboration at the Museum. Examining the life and career of Shawn through the Denishawn Era, Ted Shawn and His Men Dancers, and Jacob's Pillow, the exhibition featured original sets and costumes, artifacts, film, posters, and photographs. *Merce Cunningham: Points in Time*, in 1993, showcased Cunningham's extraordinary body of work and his collaborations with artists such as John Cage, Frank Stella, Jasper Johns, Marcel Duchamp, Andy Warhol, and Robert Rauschenberg from the 1940s to the 1990s. Original works of art including sets, backdrops, and costumes were featured, in addition to sound recordings, video, posters, photographs, and even Andy Warhol's *Silver Clouds.*[21]

FACING PAGE:

A Museum visitor reading the Merce Cunningham Hall of Fame panel honoring the 1993 inductee while Andy Warhol's *Silver Clouds,* used in Cunningham's dance work *RainForest* (1968), float in the background.

CLOCKWISE FROM TOP LEFT:

The 1993 exhibition *Merce Cunningham: Points in Time* was curated by Norton Owen and designed by Kevan Moss.

Costumes from Ted Shawn's *The Siamese Ballet* (1922) and *Cuadro Flamenco* (1923) displayed in the 1991 exhibition *Ted Shawn: A Centennial Tribute to the Father of American Dance.*

Left to right, costumes from Ted Shawn's *Valse Directoire* (1915), *The Siamese Ballet* (1922), and *Cuadro Flamenco* (1923). The wig on the floor was Shawn's demon wig from *Momiji-Gari* (1926).

Drawn in part from the personal archive of the dancer and choreographer, *Bronislava Nijinska: Classic on the Edge*, mounted in 1994, also notably presented original works of art in costume and set designs, rare photographs, memorabilia, and film. The subsequent collaborations between Owen and Moss included *Paul Taylor: In His Own Words* (1995), *The Dance Heroes of José Limón* (1997), which Owen first developed for the New York Public Library for the Performing Arts, and *Anna Sokolow: The Rebellious Spirit* (1998).[22]

LEFT TOP TO BOTTOM:
Costumes from Bronislava Nijinska's seminal 1923 ballet *Les Noces*.

Poster design by Alexandra Exter for Nijinska's ballet company Théâtre Choréographique Nijinska.

RIGHT:
Bronislava Nijinska: Classic on the Edge exhibition designer Kevan Moss and curator Norton Owen at the 1994 Museum gala.

FACING PAGE, CLOCKWISE FROM TOP LEFT:
The 1995 exhibition *Paul Taylor: In His Own Words* was curated by Norton Owen and designed by Kevan Moss.

Costumes from Taylor's *Insects and Heroes* (1961).

The Dance Heroes of José Limón was curated by Norton Owen for the New York Public Library for the Performing Arts and traveled to the Museum in 1997 for display coinciding with Limón's Hall of Fame induction that year. Kevan Moss designed the exhibition for the Museum's installation.

Costume from Limón's *The Emperor Jones* (1956).

Costumes from Limón's *The Traitor* (1954).

Costumes from Taylor's *Big Bertha* (1970).

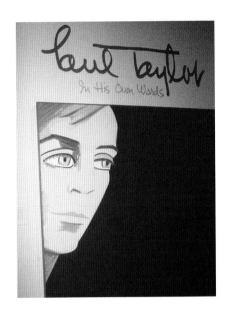

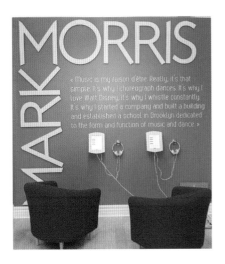

The schedule of extensive year-long exhibitions returned to the Hall of Fame program in the 2010s with installations dedicated to honorees such as Gene Kelly, Jacques d'Amboise, Rudolf Nureyev, Gregory Hines, and Patricia Wilde. In 2015, the Museum mounted a major retrospective on the career of Mark Morris that highlighted his extraordinary contributions to the art form as a dancer, choreographer, director, conductor, musician, and community leader. Mark Morris Dance Group, artistic collaborations, seminal works, and the Mark Morris Dance Center in Brooklyn were explored through a large collection of artifacts, costumes, and photographs loaned from the Dance Group. At his Hall of Fame induction, Morris described the Museum as a "fabulous and unusual and needed museum." [23]

FACING PAGE:
Mark Morris, Nancy Umanoff, Raul P. Martinez, and Laura DiRado tour *A Tribute to Mark Morris* before his Hall of Fame induction at the *¡Tango!* gala, August 8, 2015.

CLOCKWISE FROM TOP LEFT:
Costumes, set pieces, and artifacts donated by Mark Morris Dance Group upon Morris's induction into the Hall of Fame.

A listening station was installed within the exhibition that featured Morris's hour-long web radio program series *Music I Want You to Hear.*

The Museum's exhibitions coordinator and designer Laura DiRado with Mark Morris and Nancy Umanoff, executive director of Mark Morris Dance Group.

CHAPTER THREE

The Collection

The original proposal for the creation of the Museum and its initial set of by-laws established that the procurement of artifacts for the permanent collection was to focus primarily on Hall of Fame inductees.[1] The collection would thereby reflect and serve as a record of the individual history and development of the institution. Over the past thirty years, the collection has proliferated within these guidelines and further evolved to include materials from exhibitions mounted at the Museum as well as items of consequence to the considerable history of dance. At present, the Museum's repository is composed of several established collections of note in addition to independent artifacts, categorized as either objects or archival materials. A comprehensive library of dance books and periodicals comprises the Museum's resource collection.

FACING PAGE:
Detail of costume worn by Arthur Mitchell as Othello in *Prologue* (1967), choreography by Jacques d'Amboise, costume designed by Peter Larkin and executed by Karinska. Gift of NYCB.

THE COLLECTION

Objects include costumes, set pieces, and works of fine art. Costumes from myriad artists and dance companies such as Alvin Ailey American Dance Theater, Irma Duncan, Mark Morris Dance Group, and Ruth St. Denis constitute the majority of the objects in the collection. Archival materials perhaps best articulate the increasing diversity and range of the collection and encompass correspondence, photographs, audio-visual materials, books, playbills, season programs, posters, and scrap-books. Thousands of photographs form the foundation of the archive and serve as critical documentation of American dance, including images of early, retired, or lost dance works; costume design; artists; and performance. The range of photographers represented includes

LEFT:
Poster for Phyllis Lamhut Dance Company at the Theater of the Riverside Church, 1978.

RIGHT, CLOCKWISE FROM TOP LEFT:
Alice Young, George Balanchine, and Joan McCracken at the School of American Ballet, 1934, from a scrapbook. BALANCHINE is a Trademark of The George Balanchine Trust. Gift of Heidi Vosseler.

Heidi Vosseler, Balanchine, and Lucia Davidova at a picnic at the home of Alice Delamar, circa 1934, from a scrapbook. BALANCHINE is a Trademark of The George Balanchine Trust. Gift of Heidi Vosseler.

Poster for Dance Theatre of Harlem at the Apollo Theatre, designed by the artist Hilary Knight, 2001.

Ballets Jooss program, cover by "Hap" Hadley Studio, 1933.

Ballet Russe de Monte Carlo program, cover by Henri Matisse, 1939.

Dick Day, Balanchine, and Alfred Newman in Hollywood during the filming of *The Goldwyn Follies* (1938), circa 1937, from a scrapbook. BALANCHINE is a Trademark of The George Balanchine Trust. Gift of Heidi Vosseler.

THIS PAGE, LEFT TO RIGHT:

Sylvia Giselle as the Heroine and William Dollar as the Villain in *Alma Mater* (1934), choreography by George Balanchine, costumes by John Held Jr., The American Ballet, 1934. ©The George Balanchine Trust.

Charles Laskey as the Hero and Heidi Vosseler as the Dream Bride in *Alma Mater* (1934), choreography by George Balanchine, costumes by John Held Jr., The American Ballet, 1934. ©The George Balanchine Trust.

CLOCKWISE FROM TOP LEFT:
The Village by Japanese artist Yasuhide Kobashi.

Ballet Dancers by George Gách, bronze, 1980. Gift of Beau R. Peelle.

Dancing Group by George Gách, bronze, 1982. Gift of Beau R. Peelle.

The Dance by American artist Helen Levin, acrylic on canvas. Gift of Helen Levin.

Rudolf Nureyev bronze head sculpture by American artist Rose Shecht Miller. Gift of Rose Shecht Miller.

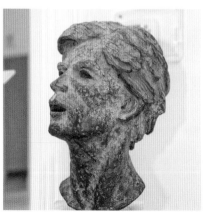

trailblazers such as Barbara Morgan, Max Waldman, Cris Alexander, Maurice Seymour, Fred Fehl, Carolyn George, Steven Caras, Paul Kolnik, and Martha Swope. Other archival highlights are season programs from an array of dance companies such as American Ballet Theatre, NYCB, and Ballet Russe de Monte Carlo. Not only are such programs a representation of the cultural zeitgeist, but evidence of the long-held tradition of synergy between dance and visual art. In concert with future exhibitions and education initiatives, the Museum aims to further explore and promote the tremendous scope of the art form through the continued, measured growth of its collection.

CLOCKWISE FROM TOP LEFT:
Ballet (1951) written and illustrated by Cecil Beaton.

Das Mary Wigman-Werk (1933) by Rudolf Bach, inscribed by Mary Wigman on March 8, 1933 to American concert promoter, Howard E. Potter, from the collection of Hanya Holm. Gift of Karen Holm Trautlein.

November 10, 1929 letter from Bill "Bojangles" Robinson to his student, Pauline Sapanara. Gift of Joe Kimpel.

Photograph of Bill "Bojangles" Robinson inscribed to his student, Pauline Sapanara, 1929. Gift of Joe Kimpel.

CLOCKWISE FROM TOP LEFT:
Traveling trunk owned by Anna Pavlova. Gift of Hannah Skye.

Dress worn by Anna Pavlova. Gift of Alissa Tschetter-Siedschlaw.

Kimono worn by Ruth St. Denis in *Omika* (1913), costume designed by St. Denis. Gift of Alison Moore and Mark Rucker.

Ballet slippers worn by Rudolf Nureyev. Gift of the Rudolf Nureyev Dance Foundation.

Headpiece worn by American Ballet Theatre principal dancer Eleanor D'Antuono in *La Sylphide* (1964/1971), choreography by Harald Lander from the original by August Bournonville, restaged in 1971 by Erik Bruhn, costumes designed by Robert O'Hearn. Gift of Eleanor D'Antuono.

Ballet slipper worn by Marcel Marceau.

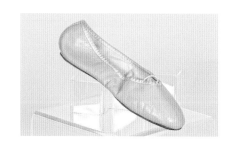

CLOCKWISE FROM LEFT:

Costume worn by Jerome Robbins for a student production, designed and made by his Aunt Gert. Gift of Sonia Robbins Cullinen.

Teaching skirt and leotard worn by Patricia Wilde, designed by Gilda Marx. Gift of Patricia Wilde.

Kimono worn by Doris Humphrey during the Denishawn Orient tour, circa 1925.

Detail of costume from *Revelations* (1960), choreography by Alvin Ailey, original costumes designed by Lawrence Maldonado, revival costumes designed by Ves Harper, "Rocka My Soul" costumes redesigned by Barbara Forbes. Gift of Alvin Ailey American Dance Theater.

Signed Converse All Star Low Top sneakers worn by Ben Vereen. Gift of Ben Vereen.

Signed pointe shoes worn by Patricia Wilde. Gift of Patricia Wilde.

Karole Armitage

Representing the Museum's most recent accession, the Karole Armitage collection comprises nine costumes from the dancer-choreographer's groundbreaking, forty-year career as an innovator and influencer in the genres of ballet and modern dance. The collection spans dance works from 1986 to 2013 and features designs by longtime collaborators David Salle, Alba Clemente, and Christian Lacroix. Included are two garments created by fashion and costume designer Peter Speliopoulos for *Fables on Global Warming*, a piece choreographed by Armitage in 2013 for her company, Armitage Gone! Dance. *Fables on Global Warming* was first introduced to an audience at the Skidmore College Dance Theater in Saratoga Springs as a work-in-progress. In 2015, the Museum presented *Making Art Dance*, a major exhibition from Mana Contemporary that explored Armitage's dynamic collaborations with visual artists. Costumes, performance video, and set pieces, such as Jeff Koons's giant inflatable pig for *Contempt* (1989), illustrated Armitage's intrinsic relationship with contemporary art.

FACING PAGE:
Karole Armitage and costume designer Peter Speliopoulos at the opening of *Making Art Dance*, June 21, 2015.

ABOVE:
Costume from *The Elizabethan Phrasing of the Late Albert Ayler* (1986), choreography by Karole Armitage, costumes by David Salle. Gift of Karole Armitage.

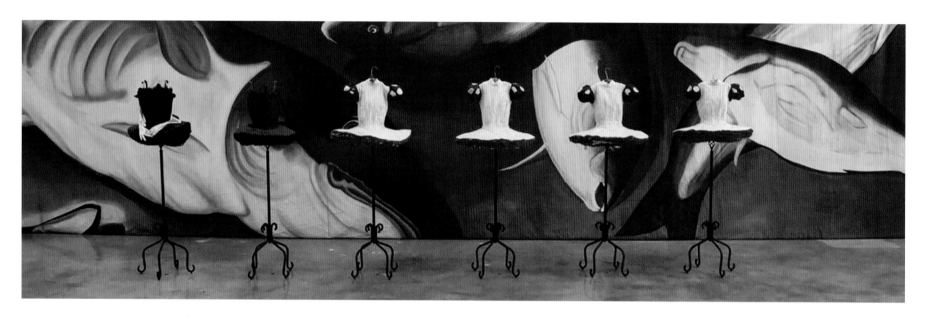

FACING PAGE:

Costumes from *The Tarnished Angels* (1987), choreography by Karole Armitage, costumes by Christian Lacroix.

CLOCKWISE FROM TOP LEFT:

Costumes from *Made in Naples* (2009), choreography by Karole Armitage, costumes by Alba Clemente.

Costume from *Made in Naples* (2009), choreography by Karole Armitage, costume by Peter Speliopoulos.

Headpiece of costume from *Made in Naples* (2009), choreography by Karole Armitage, costume by Alba Clemente.

Costume from *Fables on Global Warming* (2013), choreography by Karole Armitage, costume by Peter Speliopoulos.

Detail of costume from *Fables on Global Warming* (2013), choreography by Karole Armitage, costume by Peter Speliopoulos.

Detail of costume from *Made in Naples* (2009), choreography by Karole Armitage, costume by Alba Clemente.

Photos of installation view from *Making Art Dance* exhibition at Mana Contemporary, Jersey City, New Jersey.

Cris Alexander and Shaun O'Brien

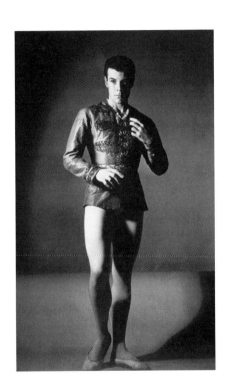

Celebrated portrait photographer and actor Cris Alexander and venerable NYCB dancer Shaun O'Brien first visited Saratoga Springs in 1966 during NYCB's premiere summer season at SPAC. They moved to Saratoga Springs permanently in 1991 after O'Brien's retirement from ballet, and for twenty years were vital members of the arts community and great friends of the Museum. After a remarkable sixty-two years as a couple, they passed away in 2012 less than two weeks apart. Alexander was one of the most sought-after portraitists of his generation and captured countless luminaries from Truman Capote and Twiggy to Gloria Vanderbilt and Mother Teresa. He also photographed some of the most acclaimed dancers and choreographers of the time including Martha Graham, Jerome Robbins, and of course, O'Brien. These tremendously compelling images, which number in the hundreds, in part comprise the collection given to the Museum in 2015 by Ralph A. Crocker and Michael P. Whitten, and featured in the Art in the Foyer series that year. Highlights include iconic photographs of George Balanchine and a host of NYCB dancers in New York and on tour. Alexander also notably documented Rudolf Nureyev's visit to the Museum in 1988 for a dinner in his honor, hosted by his close friends, Mr. and Mrs. Cornelius Vanderbilt Whitney.[2]

FACING PAGE:
Shaun O'Brien as Herr Drosselmeier in *George Balanchine's The Nutcracker*® (1954), choreography by George Balanchine, costumes by Karinska, masks by Lawrence Vlady, 1976. ©The George Balanchine Trust.

ABOVE LEFT TO RIGHT:
Shaun O'Brien in *Pas de Dix* (1955), choreography by George Balanchine, costumes by Esteban Francés. ©The George Balanchine Trust. Gift of Ralph A. Crocker and Michael P. Whitten.

Cris Alexander, self-portrait in his studio, 1980. Gift of Ralph A. Crocker and Michael P. Whitten.

CLOCKWISE FROM TOP LEFT:
Jacques d'Amboise, 1970.

George Balanchine, 1952. BALANCHINE is a Trademark of The George Balanchine Trust.

Shaun O'Brien on the lawn at SPAC, circa late 1960s.

Jerome Robbins, 1945.

Melissa Hayden in an Edith Head design, 1970.

Martha Graham, 1948.

FACING PAGE:
Shaun O'Brien and Cris Alexander.

All photos gift of Ralph A. Crocker and Michael P. Whitten.

CLOCKWISE FROM TOP LEFT:
Shaun O'Brien, Rudolf Nureyev, and Merrill Ashley at the Museum, August 1, 1988.

Shaun O'Brien with hand laundry backstage at SPAC, 1974.

O'Brien and Alexander in the woods.

Alexander and O'Brien.

FACING PAGE:
Shaun O'Brien at home in Saratoga Springs.

All photos gift of Ralph A. Crocker and Michael P. Whitten.

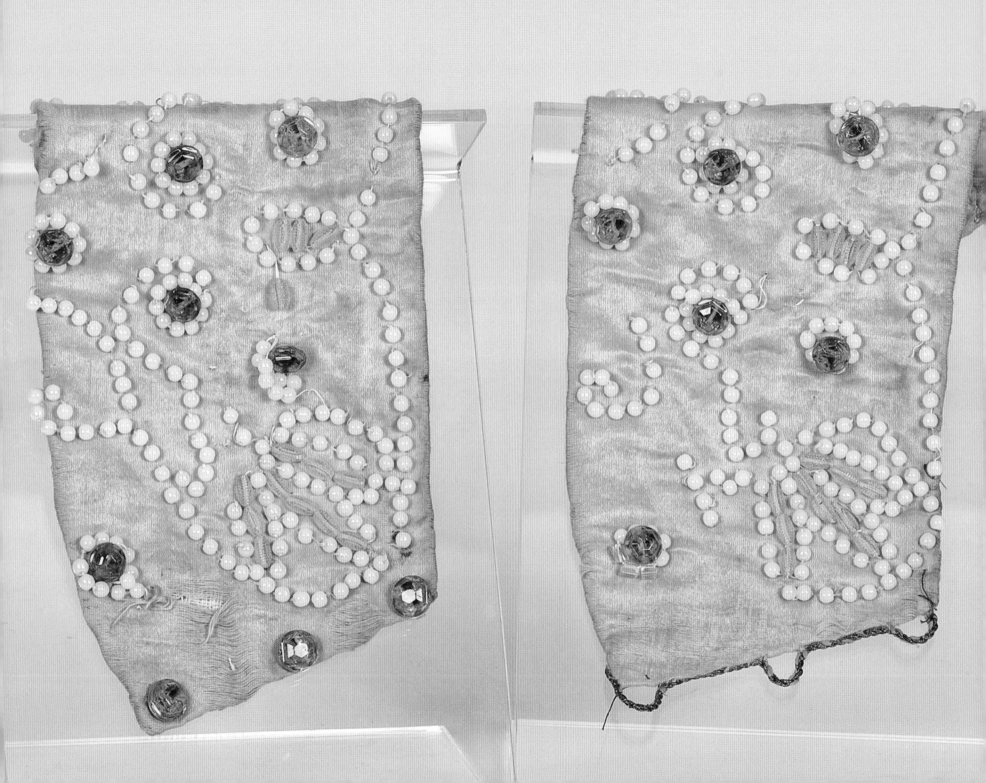

Vera Kregal

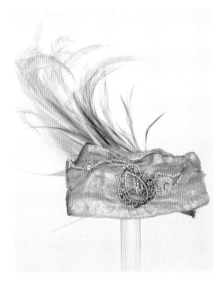

In 2003, the Museum received a selection of costume pieces and dance-wear owned by Vera Kregal, a dancer with the Mariinsky Ballet in the first part of the twentieth century. Beaded cuffs dating to 1908, headpieces, stockings, undergarments, and pointe shoes comprise this noteworthy collection donated by Kregal's great-niece, Heidi Billittier. These pieces formed the basis for discourse on the history of Russian ballet within the 2009 exhibition, *Ballets Russes,* that celebrated the centenary of the founding of Sergei Diaghilev's visionary, Paris-based company. The entire exhibition was drawn from the Museum collection and archives, and in addition to the Kregal garments, included an evening dress worn by Anna Pavlova, original photographs, and a range of programs from Diaghilev's Ballets Russes and the troupes born from it including the Ballet Russe de Monte Carlo.

FACING PAGE:
Beaded silk cuffs worn by Vera Kregal of the Mariinsky Ballet, 1908. Gift of Heidi Billittier.

TOP:
Headpieces with netting, beading, and feathers worn by Vera Kregal, circa 1920. Gift of Heidi Billittier.

BOTTOM:
Embroidered silk stockings worn by Vera Kregal of the Mariinsky Ballet. Gift of Heidi Billittier.

THE COLLECTION

Les Ballets Trockadero de Monte Carlo

The renowned all-male comic ballet company, Les Ballets Trockadero de Monte Carlo, was founded in 1974 in New York City by dancers Natch Taylor, Peter Anastos, and Antony Bassae. Over the course of more than forty years, the troupe has built a repertory that features both classical ballet and modern works, performed with singular artistry, in drag and on pointe. The enormous popularity of the Trocks is international in its scope, and to date the company has performed in more than five hundred cities in thirty-three countries. In 2014, co-founder and former artistic director Natch Taylor donated a substantial collection of artifacts to the Museum from Les Ballets Trockadero de Monte Carlo including dozens of performance and international tour posters, original photographs, performance videos, personal correspondence, program notes, playbills, and publicity materials from 1974 to 1990. Taylor also donated an important collection of over seventy issues of the performing and visual arts journal *Comœdia Illustré*, dating from 1909 to 1914.

FACING PAGE:
Poster for Les Ballets Trockadero de Monte Carlo at City Center. Gift of Natch Taylor.

CLOCKWISE FROM TOP LEFT:
Comœdia Illustré, May 1, 1912, cover design by Léon Bakst. Gift of Natch Taylor.

Poster for Les Ballets Trockadero de Monte Carlo with photo by John L. Murphy. Gift of Natch Taylor.

Rehearsal photo of co-founder and artistic director Natch Taylor. Gift of Natch Taylor.

Les Ballets Trockadero de Monte Carlo in *Don Quixote*, from left: Zamarina Zamarkova, Alexis Ivanovitch Lermontov, Euginia Repelskii, Natasha Veceslova, Olga Tchikaboumskaya, and Ida Neversayneva. Gift of Natch Taylor.

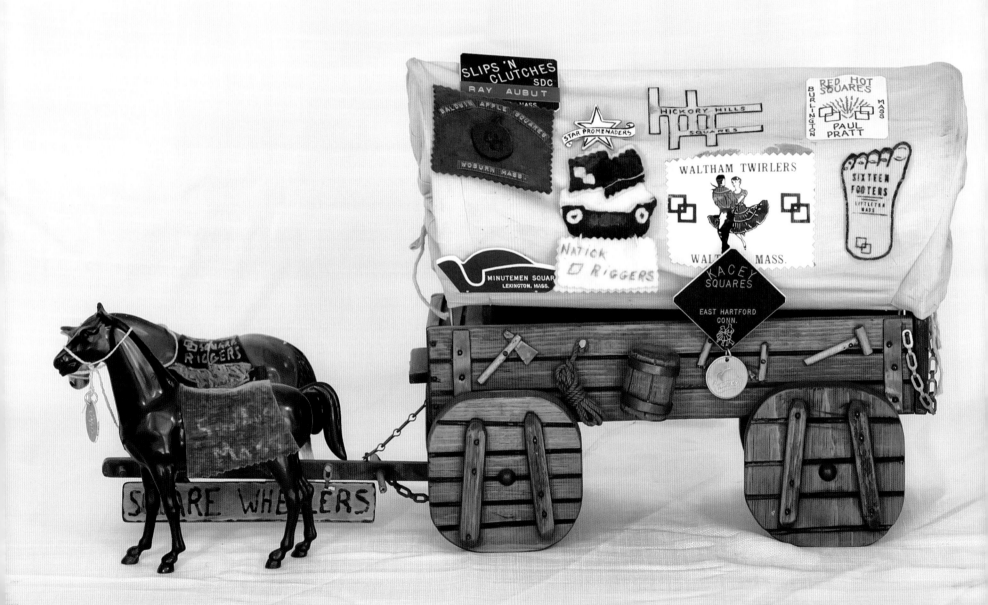

Square Dance Foundation of New England

Established in 1973, the Square Dance Foundation of New England was created to preserve the vibrant history of both folk and square dance in the twentieth century and beyond. For more than forty years, the Foundation amassed a substantial documentation of American square dance including oral histories, recordings, books, and photographs. In 2016, at the closing of the Foundation's library and museum, a large group of objects was given to the Museum. This vast selection of artifacts was the first example of square dance in the collection and a great enhancement to its holdings of social dance. Costumes and accessories, club memorabilia and scrapbooks, square dance caller recordings, historical research, photographs, and trophies in part comprise the accession. A complete set of the American Square Dance Society's official magazine, *Sets in Order,* from 1948 to 1985 was also part of the gift, an essential reference for understanding the development and evolution of square dance and its significance within the context of American life and culture.[3]

FACING PAGE:
Traveling trophy from the Square Wheelers Square Dance Club of Acton, Massachusetts, circa 1970s. Gift of the Square Dance Foundation of New England.

LEFT:
Karman western shirt, circa 1953, and Pioneer Wear suede fringed jacket. Red and white cotton homemade square dance dress. Gift of the Square Dance Foundation of New England.

FACING PAGE:
Frye red and white leather cowboy boots. Gift of the Square Dance Foundation of New England.

CLOCKWISE FROM LEFT:
Square dance couple costumes including blue cotton homemade square dance dress, matching homemade yellow vests with state of Massachusetts patches, and male shirt by Stedler's. Gift of the Square Dance Foundation of New England.

Blue leather "promenaders," circa 1984. Gift of the Square Dance Foundation of New England.

Bolo tie with hummingbird motif. Gift of the Square Dance Foundation of New England.

American Ballet Theatre

In 2011, the Museum presented the sweeping retrospective, *American Ballet Theatre: Then and Now*. Curator and former American Ballet Theatre dancer Denise Warner Limoli selected an array of costumes, programs, artifacts, and photographs to articulate the history of the company including its legendary artistic directors and signature productions. Featured objects included costumes worn by Alicia Markova and Mikhail Baryshnikov, as well as the Queen Mother costume from *Swan Lake* (1967), worn exclusively by the company's co-founder and director Lucia Chase until her retirement in 1980. This exhibition coincided with the Hall of Fame induction of award-winning set designer and co-director of American Ballet Theatre Oliver Smith.[4] At the completion of the exhibition, the Museum was given thirteen costumes on permanent loan. These costumes, in addition to original photographs, and a vast range of programs from American Ballet Theatre and its predecessor Ballet Theatre, comprise the majority of the collection. Several personal objects such as passports and scrapbooks from Lucia Chase were given to the Museum in 1992 by Lois Doherty-Mander, executive director of the Lucia Chase Foundation.[5]

FACING PAGE:

Beaded, gold-trimmed black velvet gown worn exclusively by Lucia Chase as the Queen Mother in *Swan Lake* (1967), choreography by David Blair from the original by Marius Petipa and Lev Ivanov, costume designed by Freddy Wittop and executed by Grace Costumes, New York. Gift of American Ballet Theatre.

CLOCKWISE FROM LEFT:

Sleeve detail, headpiece, and bodice detail from the Queen Mother costume from *Swan Lake* (1967), choreography by David Blair from the original by Marius Petipa and Lev Ivanov, costume designed by Freddy Wittop and executed by Grace Costumes, New York. Gift of American Ballet Theatre.

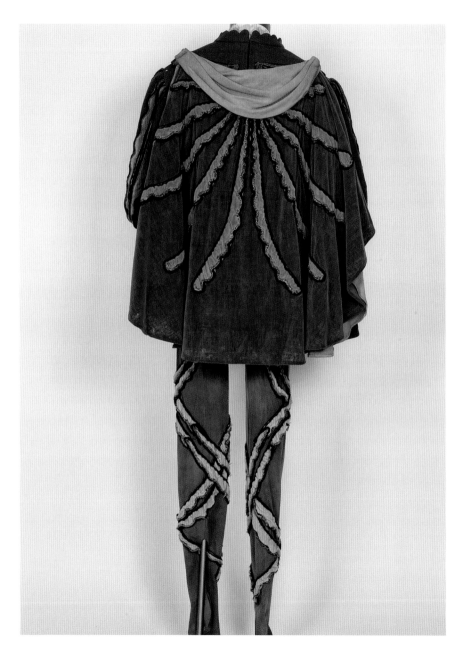

FACING PAGE LEFT TO RIGHT:

Costume worn by Antony Tudor and R. Bryce Marks as Tybalt in *Romeo and Juliet* (1943), choreography by Antony Tudor, costume by Eugene Berman. Gift of American Ballet Theatre.

Wedding dress worn by Alicia Markova as Leonor in *Don Domingo de Don Blas* (1942), choreography by Léonide Massine, costume by Julio Castillanos. Gift of American Ballet Theatre.

CLOCKWISE FROM LEFT:

Dress worn by Alicia Markova as Leonor in *Don Domingo de Don Blas* (1942), choreography by Léonide Massine, costume by Julio Castillanos. Gift of American Ballet Theatre.

Dress worn by Annabelle Lyon and Leslie Brown as the Youngest Sister in *Pillar of Fire* (1942), choreography by Antony Tudor, costume designed by Jo Mielziner and executed by Barbara Matera. Gift of American Ballet Theatre.

Theatre Guild School class notebook from 1926 and personal passports in case owned by Lucia Chase. Gift of Lois Doherty-Mander.

Dress for the young Lizzie Borden (The Accused) in *Fall River Legend* (1948), choreography by Agnes de Mille, costume by Miles White. Gift of American Ballet Theatre.

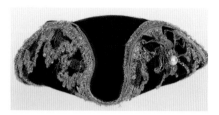

LEFT, CLOCKWISE FROM TOP LEFT:
Costume worn by Ivan Nagy and Mikhail Baryshnikov as Prince Désiré in *The Sleeping Beauty* (1976), choreography by Mary Skeaping from the original by Marius Petipa and the staging of Nicholas Sergeyev, costume by Oliver Messel.

Tricorne hat worn by Ivan Nagy and Mikhail Baryshnikov as Prince Désiré in *The Sleeping Beauty* (1976), choreography by Mary Skeaping from the original by Marius Petipa and the staging of Nicholas Sergeyev, costume by Oliver Messel.

Detail of sash and velvet jacket worn by Ivan Nagy and Kevin McKenzie as Count Albrecht in *Giselle* (ABT premiere 1940, restaged 1946 and 1968) in the 1970s, choreography by Anton Dolin after the original by Jean Coralli, costume by Peter Hall.

RIGHT:
Black velvet cape worn by Ivan Nagy and Kevin McKenzie as Count Albrecht in *Giselle* (ABT premiere 1940, restaged 1946 and 1968) in the 1970s, choreography by Anton Dolin after the original by Jean Coralli, costume by Peter Hall.

Costumes gift of American Ballet Theatre.

CLOCKWISE FROM LEFT:

1949-1950 season program for Ballet Theatre, cover art by Marcel Vertes.

1960-1961 season program for American Ballet Theatre, cover art by Marcel Vertes.

1953-1954 season program, cover art is a costume sketch for *Aleko* (1942, restaged 1953) by Marc Chagall, choreography by Léonide Massine, costumes by Marc Chagall.

1951-1952 season program, cover art is the painting *Reflection* by Paul Cadmus (1944).

Malcolm McCormick

Malcolm McCormick cultivated his career in New York as a costume designer for ballet, modern dance, and theater while simultaneously pursuing a career as a dancer beginning in the late 1940s. His earliest commissions included costumes for the Metropolitan Opera, for which he danced for nearly a decade. His first designs for modern dance, the genre for which he would receive his greatest notoriety, included Joyce Trisler's *The Bewitched: A Dance Satire* (1959) and José Limón's *The Demon* (1963). McCormick went on to establish the design program in the dance department at the University of California, Los Angeles (UCLA) in 1968 and forged a career as a respected lecturer and writer on dance.[6] In 2016, McCormick gave the Museum a substantial collection of more than two hundred and fifty costume sketches representing the entire scope of his career, from his first designs for the United Scenic Artists exam in the early 1950s to commissioned work for companies such as Ballet Souffle, Repertory Theater of Lincoln Center, Pennsylvania Ballet, and Pilobolus; work created for students and visiting artists at UCLA; and designs for choreographers such as Murray Louis. The collection also includes set designs and dozens of photographs of his costumes realized and in performance. These pieces comprised the Museum's Art in the Foyer exhibition, *Design for Dance: The Malcolm McCormick Collection*, in the thirtieth anniversary season. McCormick curated the very first exhibition at the Museum in the 1986 preview season, *Dressing the Ballet: Costumes from America's Most Celebrated Companies*.

FACING PAGE:
Malcolm McCormick's first costume sketch for ballet at age fifteen, circa 1942.

ABOVE LEFT AND RIGHT:
Male and female costume designs submitted to Jerome Robbins but never used for his ballet, *In the Night* (1970), performed by NYCB. Gift of Malcolm McCormick.

CLOCKWISE FROM TOP LEFT:
Original female costume design for *Untitled* (1975), choreography by Pilobolus. Gift of Malcolm McCormick.

Costume design for the Mama Elephant in *Carnival of the Animals*, choreography by Zachary Solov. Gift of Malcolm McCormick.

Costume design for the Chicken in *Carnival of the Animals*, choreography by Zachary Solov. Gift of Malcolm McCormick.

Costume design for the Donkey in *Carnival of the Animals*, choreography by Zachary Solov. Gift of Malcolm McCormick.

Female costume design for the Repertory Theater of Lincoln Center production of *Mary Stuart* (1971). Gift of Malcolm McCormick.

Male costume design for the Repertory Theater of Lincoln Center production of *Mary Stuart* (1971). Gift of Malcolm McCormick.

CLOCKWISE FROM TOP LEFT:

Costume design for *Zar* (circa 1970s), choreography by Margalit Oved while a visiting artist at UCLA. Gift of Malcolm McCormick.

Costume design for *Zar* (circa 1970s), choreography by Margalit Oved while a visiting artist at UCLA. Gift of Malcolm McCormick.

Female costume design with fabric swatches for a Renaissance music production by The Clarion Society, circa 1977. Gift of Malcolm McCormick.

Male costume design with fabric swatches for a Renaissance music production by The Clarion Society, circa 1977. Gift of Malcolm McCormick.

Female costume design for a dance work initially titled *Sunset Boulevard* (circa 1970s), choreography by Murray Louis while a visiting artist at UCLA. Gift of Malcolm McCormick.

Male costume design for a dance work initially titled *Sunset Boulevard* (circa 1970s), choreography by Murray Louis while a visiting artist at UCLA. Gift of Malcolm McCormick.

Steven Caras

Steven Caras began his professional life at NYCB as both a dancer and a photographer. He was granted rare and complete access to document the company in performance and in the studio by his mentor George Balanchine, beginning in the 1970s. Considered one of America's eminent dance photographers, Caras's perspective as a dancer—distinct timing and musicality and discrete knowledge of the art form—is integral to his technique and artistry behind the camera. In addition to his record of NYCB, he has captured numerous influential troupes including Miami City Ballet, Pilobolus, White Oak Dance Project, Pacific Northwest Ballet, and STREB EXTREME ACTION. In 2000, Caras curated a major exhibition of his work at the Museum that reflected the full range of his twenty-three-year career to date. *An American Mosaic: Dance Photos by Steven Caras* featured nearly one hundred, color and black and white photographs of these companies and others such as the Joffrey Ballet, MOMIX, Ballet Florida, and Paul Taylor Dance Company, and documentation of artists including Mikhail Baryshnikov, Twyla Tharp, and Natalia Makarova. His iconic 1982 image of Balanchine, *Last Bow*, was a highlight of the installation. At the close of *An American Mosaic*, Caras gave thirty-eight color prints to the Museum.

FACING PAGE:
The 2000 exhibition, *An American Mosaic: Dance Photos by Steven Caras*.
Gift of Steven Caras, 2017, ©Steven Caras, all rights reserved.

ABOVE:
A student from the School of American Ballet viewing the exhibition, *An American Mosaic: Dance Photos by Steven Caras*. Gift of Steven Caras, 2017, ©Steven Caras, all rights reserved.

CLOCKWISE FROM TOP LEFT:
Vessel (1999) with Lisa Rinehart (guest), Raquel Aedo, and Emily Coates, choreography by Amy O'Brien, White Oak Dance Project, 2000, West Palm Beach, Florida. Gift of Steven Caras, 2017, ©Steven Caras, all rights reserved.

La Petite Nutcracker Suite with Daniel Buskirk or Anna Komdanska in the *Russian Dance* costume, choreography by Victor Trevino, Les Ballets Grandiva, 1997, New York, New York. Gift of Steven Caras, 2017, ©Steven Caras, all rights reserved.

Stars and Stripes (1958) with Wendy Whelan and Igor Zelensky, choreography by George Balanchine, NYCB, 1995, New York, New York. ©The George Balanchine Trust. Gift of Steven Caras, 2017, ©Steven Caras, all rights reserved.

FACING PAGE:
Baker's Dozen (1979), choreography by Twyla Tharp, Twyla Tharp Dance Company, 1981, Nashville, Tennessee. Gift of Steven Caras, 2017, ©Steven Caras, all rights reserved.

Eleo Pomare

The Museum's unprecedented 2011 exhibition, *Eleo Pomare: The Man, The Artist, The Maker of Artists*, celebrated the prodigious career of Colombian-American choreographer and contemporary dance trail-blazer, Eleo Pomare. After establishing his first company in New York in 1958, Pomare left for Europe in 1962 to study with German Expressionist choreographer Kurt Jooss on a John Hay Whitney Opportunity Fellowship.[7] Prompted by the civil rights movement, from which he drew inspiration for numerous provocative dance works for the Eleo Pomare Dance Company, he returned to the United States permanently in 1964. His choreography was largely distinguished by its strong sociopolitical themes, and his performances were celebrated for their power and truth. At the close of *Eleo Pomare: The Man, The Artist, The Maker of Artists*, a large collection of artifacts from the company was given to the Museum on permanent loan. This important assemblage conveys the breadth of Pomare's artistry and includes costumes from both signature and seminal dance works such as *Missa Luba* (1965), *Las Desenamorada* (1967), *Narcissus Rising* (1968), and *Phoenix* (1987). Several works of fine art by Pomare that inspired his choreography also comprise this collection, including ink drawings and oil and watercolor paintings.

FACING PAGE:
Malcolm X (1965), oil on board with newsprint by Eleo Pomare. This painting later inspired Pomare's dance work, *Hushed Voices* (1974). Gift of Eleo Pomare Dance Company.

LEFT:
Eleo Pomare in *Resonance*, Holland.

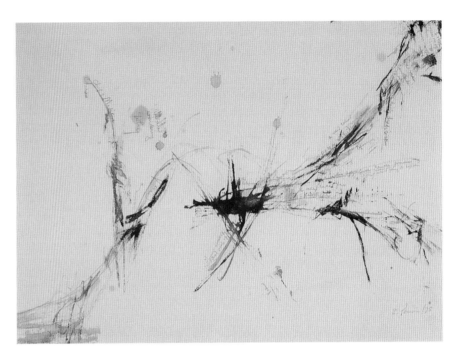

FACING PAGE:
Front and back view of costume from *Narcissus Rising* (1968), choreography and costume design by Eleo Pomare. Gift of Eleo Pomare Dance Company.

CLOCKWISE FROM LEFT:
Costume from *Roots* (1972), choreography and costume design by Eleo Pomare. Gift of Eleo Pomare Dance Company.

Costume from *Roots* (1972), choreography and costume design by Eleo Pomare. Gift of Eleo Pomare Dance Company.

Watercolor on paper by Eleo Pomare, 1975. Gift of Eleo Pomare Dance Company.

Costume pieces from *Narcissus Rising* (1968), choreography and costume design by Eleo Pomare. Gift of Eleo Pomare Dance Company.

143

Katherine S. Dreier 1934

Ted Shawn

American modern dance pioneer, Ted Shawn, was among the first group of Hall of Fame inductees in 1987, and was honored with a retrospective at the Museum in 1991, *Ted Shawn: A Centennial Tribute to the Father of American Dance*.[8] As a result, Barton Mumaw, former Men Dancer and Shawn's longtime muse and partner, donated a notable collection of books, early performance programs from Jacob's Pillow and Ted Shawn and His Men Dancers, artifacts, and original photographs of both Shawn and Mumaw in performance and at the Pillow. The Museum also includes in this collection costumes from Shawn's *Death of a God* (1929) and *Olympiad-A Suite of Sports Dances* (1936), and a notable lithograph by Katherine S. Dreier, American artist, collector, and co-founder of the Société Anonyme.[9] Dreier was a friend and patron of Shawn, and the author of *Shawn the Dancer* (1933). In 1934, she created *1 to 40 Variations*, two groups of twenty black and white lithographs with pochoir hand coloring, each one of which is unique. The Museum's lithograph was a gift of Stanley Davis, a student at Jacob's Pillow in the mid-1930s. Shawn choreographed *A Dreier Lithograph* for six dancers in 1935 to a composition by Jess Meeker, the Pillow's composer and musical director, inspired by one of Dreier's *Variations*.[10]

FACING PAGE:
1 to 40 Variations (1934), black and white lithograph with pochoir hand coloring by Katherine S. Dreier. Gift of Stanley Davis.

LEFT:
Ted Shawn, 1971. Gift of Barton Mumaw.

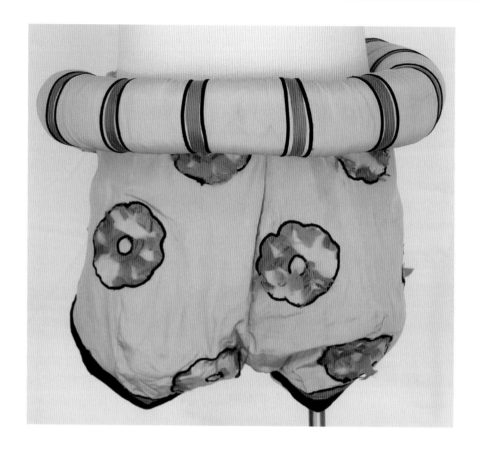

LEFT TO RIGHT:

Costume from *Death of a God* (1929), choreography by Ted Shawn.

The inaugural issue of *The Denishawn Magazine*, Vol.1, No.1, 1924.

FACING PAGE, CLOCKWISE FROM LEFT:

Barton Mumaw in *Gnossienne* (1919), choreography by Ted Shawn. Gift of Barton Mumaw.

Barton Mumaw in "The Banner Bearer" from *Olympiad – A Suite of Sports Dances* (1936). Gift of Barton Mumaw.

Shawn and His Men Dancers program for *Dance of the Ages* (1938) and *O Libertad!* (1937), circa 1939. Gift of Barton Mumaw.

Season program for *Shawn and His Men Dancers*, 1939-1940. Gift of Barton Mumaw.

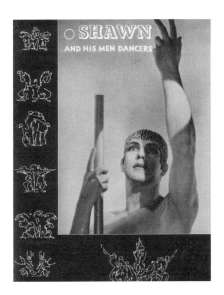

New York City Ballet

The annual residency of the NYCB at SPAC has played a fundamental role in the continued cultivation of dance audiences and the development of dance education in Saratoga Springs. Over the past thirty years, the Museum has mounted seven exhibitions solely devoted to NYCB or George Balanchine himself. Small displays on Balanchine ballets have also been created, including tributes to *Coppélia* (2009), *A Midsummer Night's Dream* (2010), and *Jewels* (2011).[11] Amassed, in part, from these myriad installations, an expansive array of artifacts from NYCB represents one of the most substantial collections at the Museum. Included is a considerable permanent loan of costumes by esteemed designers such as Barbara Karinska, Barbara Matera, Irene Sharaff, and Rouben Ter-Arutunian; well over one thousand photographs documenting NYCB from its earliest performances and its precursors such as the American Ballet and Ballet Caravan; and dozens of posters and a wide range of season programs reflecting the rich history of the company.

FACING PAGE:
Mask from *Pulcinella* (1972), choreography by George Balanchine and Jerome Robbins, costumes by Eugene Berman, masks by Kermit Love. ©The George Balanchine Trust. Gift of NYCB.

LEFT:
Costume worn by Heather Hawk and Carol Divet in *Symphony in C* (1948), choreography by George Balanchine, original costumes by Karinska. ©The George Balanchine Trust. Gift of NYCB.

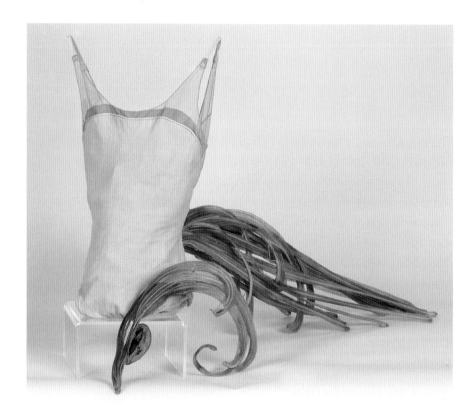

LEFT TO RIGHT:
Costume worn by Gelsey Kirkland in *The Song of the Nightingale* (1972), choreography by John Taras, costume designed by Rouben Ter-Arutunian and executed by Karinska. Gift of NYCB.

Costume from *Ballet Imperial* (Ballet Caravan premiere 1941, NYCB premiere 1964), choreography by George Balanchine, costume by Rouben Ter-Arutunian. ©The George Balanchine Trust. Gift of NYCB.

FACING PAGE, LEFT TO RIGHT:
Costume worn by Suzanne Farrell as Dulcinea in *Don Quixote* (1965), choreography by George Balanchine, costume designed by Esteban Francés and executed by Karinska. ©The George Balanchine Trust. Gift of NYCB.

Costume worn by Anne Boley, Delia Peters, and Joan Van Orden in *Bourrée Fantasque* (1949), choreography by George Balanchine, costume by Karinska. ©The George Balanchine Trust. Gift of NYCB.

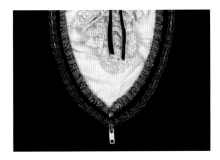

FACING PAGE, LEFT TO RIGHT:

Costume worn by Leonid Kozlov in *Swan Lake* (1951), choreography by George Balanchine, original costumes designed by Cecil Beaton (1951) and executed by Karinska, subsequent costume design by Rouben Ter-Arutunian (1964–1985) and executed by Karinska. ©The George Balanchine Trust. Gift of NYCB.

Male costume by Karinska, ballet unknown. Gift of NYCB.

CLOCKWISE FROM LEFT:

Costumes worn by Mandy-Jayne Richardson and Gloriann Hicks in *PAMTGG* (1971), choreography by George Balanchine, costumes designed by Irene Sharaff and executed by Karinska. ©The George Balanchine Trust. Gift of NYCB.

Costume worn by Peter Martins as Frantz in *Coppélia* (1974), choreography by George Balanchine and Alexandra Danilova after Marius Petipa, costume designed by Rouben Ter-Arutunian and executed by Barbara Matera. ©The George Balanchine Trust. Gift of NYCB.

Detail of costume by Karinska, worn by Francisco Moncion, ballet unknown. Gift of NYCB.

Costume worn by Bruce Wells and Bart Cook in *Pulcinella* (1972), choreography by George Balanchine and Jerome Robbins, costume designed by Eugene Berman and executed by Karinska. ©The George Balanchine Trust. Gift of NYCB.

TOP LEFT AND RIGHT:

Angel costume from *George Balanchine's The Nutcracker®* (1954), choreography by George Balanchine, costume by Karinska. ©The George Balanchine Trust. Gift of NYCB.

BOTTOM LEFT:

1954 poster for *George Balanchine's The Nutcracker®* (1954), choreography by George Balanchine, costumes by Karinska, masks by Lawrence Vlady. ©The George Balanchine Trust. Gift of NYCB.

FACING PAGE LEFT, TOP TO BOTTOM:

Hat worn by Walter Georgov as The Motorist in *Filling Station* (Ballet Caravan premiere 1938, NYCB premiere 1953), choreography by Lew Christensen, hat designed by Paul Cadmus and executed by Karinska. Gift of NYCB.

Filling Station (Ballet Caravan premiere 1938, NYCB premiere 1953), choreography by Lew Christensen, original set and costume design by Paul Cadmus.

FACING PAGE RIGHT, CLOCKWISE FROM TOP:

Hat worn by Edward Villella in *Pulcinella* (1972), choreography by George Balanchine and Jerome Robbins, costumes by Eugene Berman. ©The George Balanchine Trust. Gift of NYCB.

Ballet slippers worn and signed by Jacques d'Amboise. Gift of Lisa Akker.

Helmet worn by Joysanne Sidimus in *A Midsummer Night's Dream* (1962), choreography by George Balanchine, costumes by Karinska. ©The George Balanchine Trust. Gift of NYCB.

Helmet from *Tricolore* (1978), choreography by Peter Martins, Jean-Pierre Bonnefoux, and Jerome Robbins, costumes by Rouben Ter-Arutunian. Gift of NYCB.

Hat worn by Shaun O'Brien in *Filling Station* (Ballet Caravan premiere 1938, NYCB premiere 1953), choreography by Lew Christensen, hat designed by Paul Cadmus and executed by Karinska. Gift of NYCB.

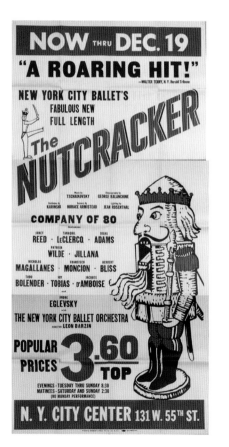

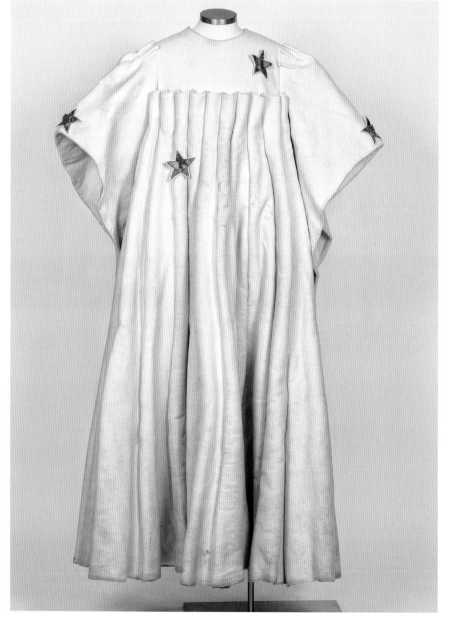

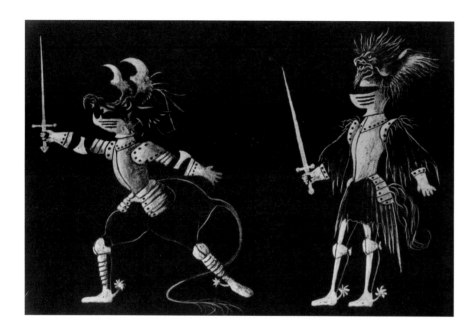

CLOCKWISE FROM TOP LEFT:
Design sketch for children's costumes in *Don Quixote* (1965), choreography by George Balanchine, mask and armor design by Lawrence Vlady. ©The George Balanchine Trust. Gift of NYCB.

Tour poster for performances from October 9 to October 22, at the Teatro di San Carlo in Naples, Italy, circa 1953. Gift of NYCB.

Child's mask and armor from *Don Quixote* (1965), choreography by George Balanchine, mask and armor design by Lawrence Vlady. ©The George Balanchine Trust. Gift of NYCB.

TEATRO DI S. CARLO

Ente Autonomo

STAGIONE D'AUTUNNO

VENERDI 9 OTTOBRE · ORE 21

Terzo spettacolo del

NEW YORK CITY BALLET

diretto da

GEORGE BALANCHINE

PROGRAMMA

CONCERTO BAROCCO

Musica di JOHANN SEBASTIAN BACH
Coreografia di GEORGE BALANCHINE   Costumi di JEAN ROSENTHAL

SINFONIA SCOZZESE

Musica di F. MENDELSSOHN - BARTHOLDY
Coreografia di GEORGE BALANCHINE   Scena di HORACE ARMISTEAD
Costumi di BARBARA KARINSKA   Effetti di luce di JEAN ROSENTHAL

Maestro Direttore
LEON BARZIN

A LA FRANCAIX

Musica di JEAN FRANCAIX
Coreografia di GEORGE BALANCHINE   Effetti di luce JEAN ROSENTHAL

BOURRÉE FANTASQUE

Musica di EMANUEL CHABRIER   Coreografia di GEORGE BALANCHINE
Costumi di BARBARA KARINSKA   Effetti di luce di JEAN ROSENTHAL

Maestro Direttore
HUGO FIORATO

PREZZI (compreso ingresso e tasse)

Poltrona I zona	L. 1000	Posto di Palco di IV fila	L. 500	
Poltrona II zona	„ 800	Galleria V fila	„ 400	
Posto di Palco di I fila	„ 700	Posto di Palco V fila	„ 300	
Posto di Palco di II fila	„ 800	Loggione VI fila	„ 200	
Posto di Palco di III fila	„ 600	Posto di Palco VI fila	„ 100	

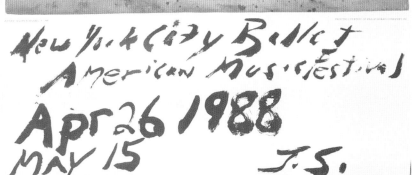

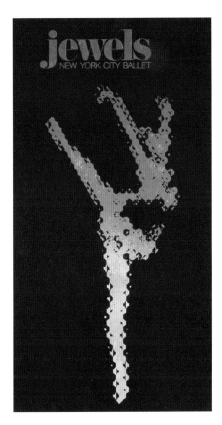

CLOCKWISE FROM LEFT:

Poster for the NYCB American Music Festival, April 26 to May 15, 1988, designed by Julian Schnabel. Gift of NYCB.

1961 season program for NYCB. Gift of NYCB.

Jewels poster, Rubies version, designed by Donn Matus, circa 1967. Gift of Ralph A. Crocker and Michael P. Whitten.

1954 season program for NYCB, cover photograph by George Platt Lynes. Gift of NYCB.

Tommy Tune

For the occasion of his 2009 Hall of Fame induction, National Medal of Arts, Drama Desk, and ten-time Tony award winner Tommy Tune offered the Museum, on temporary loan, an exceptional collection of twenty pairs of shoes and a large group of paintings and lithographs created by his own hand. This collection comprised an installation that season which honored Tune's remarkable career in theater and film as a performer, director, and choreographer, spanning some fifty-two years and continuing to this day. This collection has remained a mainstay of the permanent Hall of Fame exhibition. Worn by Tune himself on both stage and screen, the shoes reflect the great expanse of his career from the 1971 film *The Boy Friend* to Broadway's *My One and Only* (1983) to his popular 2002 revue at the Little Shubert Theater, *White Tie and Tails*. The collection also in part reflects the singular history of the Museum including shoes given to Tune by 2016 Hall of Fame inductee Gregory Hines and those worn by Tune in Kenn Duncan's series, *Red Shoes*, exhibited at the Museum in 2009.[12]

FACING PAGE:
Examples from the Museum's collection of Tommy Tune's shoes photographed for *CBS News Sunday Morning* for a June 11, 2017 segment with Tune.

LEFT:
Watercolor on paper by Tommy Tune, self-portrait in top hat. Gift of Tommy Tune.

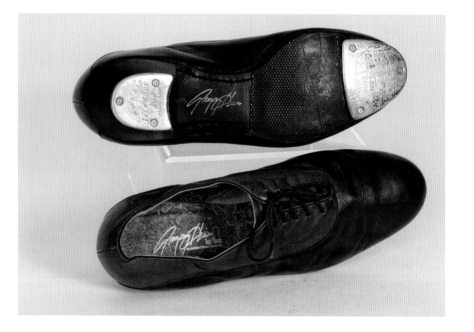

CLOCKWISE FROM TOP LEFT:
Tap shoes worn by Tommy Tune on the *Tonight Show Starring Johnny Carson*, May 15, 1973.

Tap shoes worn by Tommy Tune in the original Broadway production of *My One and Only* (1983-1985), staged and choreographed by Tommy Tune and Thommie Walsh, associate choreographer Baayork Lee, associate director Phillip Oesterman, costumes design by Rita Ryack.

Tap shoes worn by Tommy Tune in the revue *Two for the Show* (1998).

Tap shoes from the Gregory Hines collection for Capezio worn by Tommy Tune, given to him by Hines, circa 1990s.

Tap shoes worn by Tommy Tune in Kenn Duncan's book, *Red Shoes*.

Tap shoes worn by Tommy Tune in the revue *Tommy Tune Moonlighting!* (1994).

FACING PAGE:
Tap shoes worn by Tommy Tune in the film *The Boy Friend* (1971), direction by Ken Russell.

All shoes gift of Tommy Tune.

The Fugitive Gesture

The 1988 landmark exhibition, *The Fugitive Gesture: Masterpieces of Dance Photography 1849 to the Present*, was the first major installation at the Museum to present dance outside of the American landscape. Created by internationally-renowned photography curator and author William A. Ewing, *The Fugitive Gesture* considered both the art and craft of dance photography within themes of invention, record and document, icon and idol, independent eye, collaboration, and tour de force.[13] Nearly one hundred and fifty black and white photographs by notable and unknown photographers alike were featured, representing a broad range of dance genres and milieus. Works by luminaries such as George Platt Lynes, Brassaï, Ilse Bing, Irving Penn, Barbara Morgan, Lotte Jacobi, George Hoyningen-Huene, Edgar Degas, and Margaret Bourke-White, most of whom did not work exclusively in dance, were included among this vast and diverse assemblage of photographers and images. Ewing gave this complete collection of prints to the Museum on permanent loan at the end of the exhibition. *The Fugitive Gesture* was restaged in its entirety in the 2001 season.

FACING PAGE:
Walker Evans photograph of Ballet Theatre dancers in rehearsal at the Metropolitan Opera House, New York City, October 1945.

LEFT:
George Platt Lynes self-portrait at the Pierre Matisse Gallery at 41 East 57th Street, New York City, with one of his dance photographs on the far gallery wall, 1940.

Roos Family–Andrew DeVries

The 2013 exhibition, *Homage to Dance*, celebrated the work of renowned American visual artist Andrew DeVries. More than forty bronze sculptures and twenty pastel drawings were displayed in the Museum, in addition to five large-scale sculptures installed in the front garden. A foremost sculptor of dance, DeVries has garnered inspiration from studios in the United States and around the world including Alvin Ailey American Dance Theater, Pittsburgh Ballet Theatre, Académie de Danse Princesse Grace in Monaco, The Juilliard School, and Jacob's Pillow. *Homage to Dance* represented DeVries's largest exhibition to date and prompted a significant acquisition for the Museum soon thereafter. In 2015, an important collection of seven bronze sculptures by DeVries, amassed by Beverly Roos, was given to the Museum by the Roos family in her honor. Among the works are *Apollo* (2011), *Terpsichore* (1994), and *Seagull* (2004). Modeled after former Hamburg Ballet principal dancer Heather Jurgensen, *Seagull* is also installed at the Ballettzentrum Hamburg, the company's training facility and home to the School of the Hamburg Ballet.

FACING PAGE:
Nocturne (1998), bronze, from the 2013 exhibition, *Homage to Dance.*

CLOCKWISE FROM TOP LEFT:
Terpsichore (1994), bronze, 4/12 edition. Gift of the Roos Family.

Odyssey (2006), bronze, 3/12 edition. Gift of the Roos Family.

Apollo (2011), bronze, 2/8 edition. Gift of the Roos Family.

Seagull (2004), bronze, 5/12 edition. Gift of the Roos Family.

Hines

Gregory Hines was one of the most compelling and virtuosic performers of the 20th century, a thrilling and innovative tap artist, actor, singer, and choreographer. Tap dancing and its rich heritage were the essence of his life and tremendous body of work. He decidedly modernized the rhythm tap tradition and continually used his celebrity to preserve, promote, and this American art form.

Gregory Hines

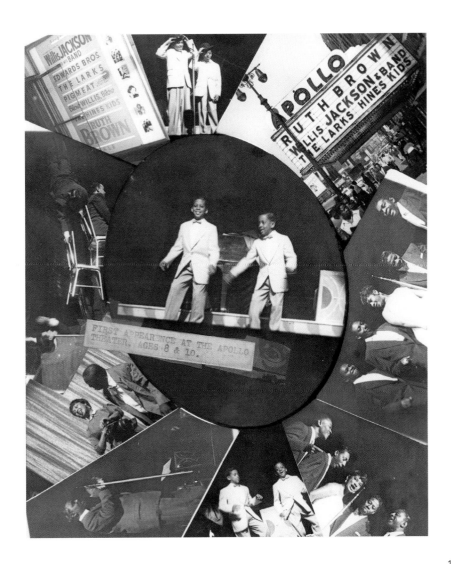

One of the most compelling and virtuosic performers of the twentieth century, Gregory Hines was an innovative tap artist, actor, singer, and choreographer on both stage and screen. Tap dancing and its deep heritage were the essence of his life and his tremendous body of work as he used his celebrity to preserve, promote, and advance the art form. In 2016, Hines was inducted into the Hall of Fame and an exhibition was created to honor his remarkable fifty-two-year career. Featured artifacts included the portable, microphoned dance floor designed and used by Hines in the 1980s; a traveling trunk that accompanied The Hines Kids, his childhood act with his brother Maurice, on tour in the 1950s; Tony award nomination cards for *Eubie!* (1978–1979), *Comin' Uptown* (1979–1980), and *Sophisticated Ladies* (1980–1981); and photographs taken by Hines, a gifted photographer in his own right, during the filming of *White Nights* (1985). At the close of the exhibition, The Gregory Hines Estate donated each one of the objects on display to the Museum on permanent loan.

FACING PAGE:
Savion Glover visiting the Hall of Fame exhibition, *A Tribute to Gregory Hines*, at *The Dancing Athlete* gala, August 13, 2016.

LEFT:
Photo collage of The Hines Kids' first appearance at the Apollo Theater, early 1950s. Gift of The Gregory Hines Estate.

CLOCKWISE FROM TOP LEFT:
Traveling trunk that accompanied The Hines Kids on tour between approximately 1952 and 1958. They officially changed their name to The Hines Brothers in 1958. Gift of The Gregory Hines Estate.

Drawing depicting Gregory Hines as Jelly Roll Morton that was given to Hines, autographed by the entire cast of *Jelly's Last Jam* including Savion Glover and Ben Vereen, circa 1993. Gift of The Gregory Hines Estate.

45 RPM vinyl record of "Early in the Morning" and "When It's All Over" by Hines, Hines & Dad, Kapp Records, 1969. Gift of The Gregory Hines Estate.

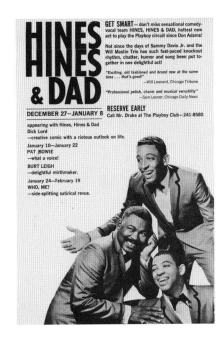

CLOCKWISE FROM TOP LEFT:

Hines, Hines & Dad promotional card for The Playboy Club, Cincinnati, Ohio, circa late 1960s. Gift of The Gregory Hines Estate.

Self-portrait taken by Gregory Hines on the street, early to mid-1980s. Gift of The Gregory Hines Estate.

Portrait taken by Gregory Hines of his *White Nights* co-star Isabella Rossellini, circa 1984. Gift of The Gregory Hines Estate.

Self-portrait taken by Gregory Hines while living in London filming *White Nights*, circa 1984. Gift of The Gregory Hines Estate.

Portrait taken by Gregory Hines of Helen Mirren during the filming of *White Nights*, circa 1984. Gift of The Gregory Hines Estate.

Tony Award Nomination Card for Gregory Hines in *Sophisticated Ladies*, 1980-81. Gift of The Gregory Hines Estate.

Paul Kolnik

Renowned American photographer, Paul Kolnik, has been capturing the performing arts in New York for more than forty years. His incomparable oeuvre includes over fifty Broadway productions such as *The Producers*, *Hairspray*, *War Horse*, and *The King and I*; symphony orchestras and artists at Carnegie Hall; and influential dance troupes including Alvin Ailey American Dance Theater, Twyla Tharp Dance, San Francisco Ballet, Martha Graham Dance Company, American Ballet Theatre, and Paul Taylor Dance Company. Beginning in 1975, his longest and most prolific association has been with NYCB, for which he remains the official photographer. His documentation of the company to date totals hundreds of thousands of images. Kolnik has collaborated with the Museum on several occasions including the creation of two digital displays of photographs of NYCB and two Art in the Foyer installations, which he has granted on permanent loan.[14] *Ballet, Broadway, and Beyond* (2009) articulated the breadth of Kolnik's work in both musical theater and dance, in a compelling juxtaposition of images from these genres. *Moment to Moment: A History of Time and Place* (2016) highlighted Kolnik's photographs of NYCB at SPAC and revealed his own deep connection as an artist to Saratoga Springs.

The original Broadway production of *Contact* (2000-2002), direction and choreography by Susan Stroman, "Girl on a Swing," Stephanie Michels with Seán Martin Hingston and Scott Taylor.

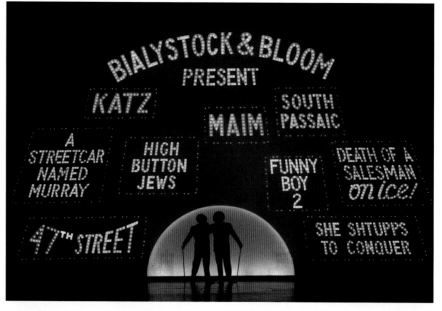

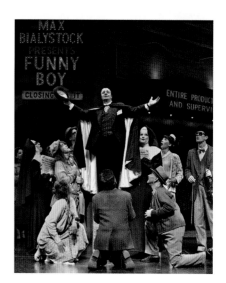

FACING PAGE, CLOCKWISE FROM LEFT:
Tommy Tune in the Off-Broadway production of *Tommy Tune: White Tie and Tails* (2002), direction and choreography by Tommy Tune with music direction by Michael Biaggi.

Matthew Broderick and Nathan Lane in the original Broadway production of *The Producers* (2001-2007), direction and choreography by Susan Stroman, based on the film by Mel Brooks.

CLOCKWISE FROM TOP LEFT:
The Four Temperaments (Ballet Society premiere 1946, NYCB premiere 1948) performed by NYCB in 2015 at SPAC, choreography by George Balanchine. ©The George Balanchine Trust.

Patricia McBride and Mikhail Baryshnikov in *The Steadfast Tin Soldier* (1975) performed by NYCB in 1978 at SPAC, choreography by George Balanchine. ©The George Balanchine Trust.

Damian Woetzel in *Prodigal Son* (Ballets Russes premiere 1929, NYCB premiere 1950) performed by NYCB in 1997 at SPAC, choreography by George Balanchine. ©The George Balanchine Trust.

Ashley Bouder and Jonathan Stafford in *The Sleeping Beauty* (1991) performed by NYCB in 2007 at SPAC, choreography by Peter Martins.

CHAPTER FOUR

The Lewis A. Swyer Studios and the School of the Arts

The final and perhaps most critical installment of the original three-phase plan of the National Museum of Dance was the construction of three state-of-the-art studios, the main vehicle through which it would function as a living museum.[1] Commitments from the New York State Summer School of the Arts (NYSSSA) Schools of Ballet and Dance in the late 1980s for their summer intensives and NYCB for additional rehearsal space during their annual residency at SPAC jumpstarted the development of these studios.[2] Lewis Swyer believed that "dance was the most creative and noble pursuit of all the performing arts" and that everyone should have the opportunity to appreciate it.[3] The presence of live dance was a founding principle of the Museum and remains fundamental to its mission. Nearly three years after his untimely passing, ground was broken in November 1991 for the Lewis A. Swyer School for the Performing Arts, named in Swyer's honor for his perseverance and unwavering vision for the completion and boundless potential of the Museum as a site for innovative arts education, collaboration, and creation.

Three-quarters of the $1 million project budget was raised in private funds by the time of the groundbreaking ceremony. Major gifts were once again secured from Mr. and Mrs. Cornelius Vanderbilt Whitney and William E. Murray, and two of the three studios were dedicated in their names. An attorney and founding board member, Murray was a stalwart supporter of the Museum during his lifetime. Among numerous philanthropic endeavors, he was a committed benefactor of the arts and served as a trustee of the Spoleto Festival USA and SPAC, and was chairman of the American Friends of the Hermitage.[4] In fact, he was so inspired by Swyer's leadership in both the arts and civil rights that in 1988 he established the Lewis Swyer Scholarship at Skidmore College in honor of his good friend.[5] The third studio was dedicated to Hanya Holm, modern dance pioneer, eminent Broadway choreographer, and Hall of Fame inductee. Holm passed away on November 3, 1992, at age ninety-nine and in her will bequeathed five percent of her estate to the Museum, which it in turn allocated toward the realization of the studios.[6]

FACING PAGE:
Museum founder Lewis A. Swyer.

LEFT:
Founding board member and a lead funder of the Studios, William E. Murray.

LEFT TO RIGHT:
Diorama for a Hanya Holm dance work created by her son, theater designer Klaus Holm. Gift of Hanya Holm.

Costume worn by Hanya Holm. Gift of Hanya Holm.

FACING PAGE:
Crandell Diehl and Hanya Holm, choreographic collaborators on the original Broadway production of *My Fair Lady* (1956), London, 1958. Gift of Hanya Holm.

Today, the Lewis A. Swyer School for the Performing Arts is known as the Lewis A. Swyer Studios, home to the Museum's School of the Arts and host to a wide breadth of Museum programming and special events, including the annual gala. Myriad residencies, workshops, and performances are held in the Studios, as well as auditions for conservatories such as the Boston Ballet School, Nutmeg Ballet Conservatory, American Academy of Ballet, Walnut Hill School for the Arts, and children's roles during NYCB's residency at SPAC. Master classes and lecture-demonstrations began in the 1986 preview season in partnership with SPAC and Skidmore College in a program titled Dance Views, featuring trailblazers such as Bella Lewitsky, Merce Cunningham, and Paul Taylor. This laid the groundwork for the type of programming that the Museum would fully engage and excel in. The completion of the Studios in the summer of 1992 enabled the Museum to launch a robust, enduring schedule of dance education initiatives and live performance with the goal of further disseminating the art form and developing a broader understanding and audience for dance in the process.

FACING PAGE:
NYCB Assistant Children's Ballet Master Arch Higgins and Children's Ballet Master Dena Abergel conducting an audition at the Studios for NYCB children's roles for performances at SPAC.

CLOCKWISE FROM TOP LEFT:
Dozens of dancers waiting to audition at the Studios for NYCB children's roles for performances at SPAC.

School of the Arts students chosen to perform in Circus Polka (1972) at SPAC, choreography by Jerome Robbins, 2014.

Local dancers waiting to audition for NYCB children's roles for performances at SPAC.

Constructing the Lewis A. Swyer Studios

Built by the L. A. Swyer Company, the 12,000-square-foot single-story structure was designed by Kurzon Architects to complement the architectural style of the original Washington Bathhouse. Its white stucco exterior with half-timber work and central dormer clearly echo the distinct façade of the Museum. In respect for its surroundings and placement within the Saratoga Spa State Park, only one tree was felled for the construction of the studios, and two wrought iron fences were erected on either end to enclose the courtyard between the studio building and the Museum.[7] In planning the interior of the facility, Kurzon Architects consulted with board member Nancy Norman Lassalle on the design of the new School of American Ballet building in Manhattan, opened in January 1991. Certain key elements were incorporated in the building plans for the Museum's studios.[8] NYSSSA School of Ballet director Heather Watts and School of Dance director Carolyn Adams were consulted on the studio and floor design, as were Peter Martins and Perry Silvey of NYCB.[9]

FACING PAGE:
Carolyn Adams, Charles Wait, Edward Swyer, Marylou Whitney, William E. Murray, and Heather Watts at the groundbreaking for the Studios, November 20, 1991.

LEFT:
Executive Director of SPAC Herb Chesbrough, board member Edward Swyer, Marylou Whitney, and founding board member Nancy Norman Lassalle at the groundbreaking ceremony.

CLOCKWISE FROM TOP LEFT:
Nancy Norman Lassalle, Marylou Whitney, and Herb Chesbrough viewing the future site of the Studios from the Museum.

The Museum's second director, Joanne Allison, at the groundbreaking for the Studios.

Marylou Whitney's hardhat for the groundbreaking ceremony.

FACING PAGE, CLOCKWISE FROM LEFT:
NYSSSA School of Dance director Carolyn Adams, Marylou Whitney, and NYSSSA School of Ballet director Heather Watts.

Herb Chesbrough, board member Charles Wait, Marylou Whitney, and Edward Swyer at the groundbreaking ceremony.

Orin Lehman, New York State Commissioner of Parks, Recreation, and Historic Preservation, at the groundbreaking.

FACING PAGE:
The foundation being laid for the Studios.

THIS PAGE:
The Studios were designed by Kurzon Architects of Albany, New York and built by the L.A. Swyer Company.

Constructed in a linear arrangement, the center studio measures forty-five feet by sixty feet, the two flanking studios each measure forty-five feet by fifty-two feet and feature a sprung floor system. All three contain twenty-two foot ceilings and abundant natural light. A folding wall system between the three studios allow for tremendous flexibility within the space and when completely open mimic the footprint of a full theater stage.[10] Each of the studios is soundproof and two-way mirrors and mono headphones allow visitors to observe classes and the choreographic process without disturbance to students and artists. The facilities also include a lobby, lounge, locker rooms, showers, and offices.

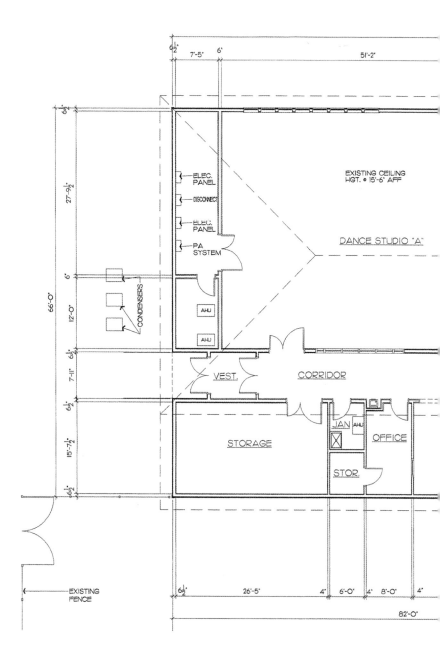

ABOVE:
Left to right, Herb Chesbrough, Marylou Whitney, and
Edward Swyer at the opening of the Studios, June 29, 1992.

RIGHT:
Floorplan for the Studios designed by Kurzon Architects.

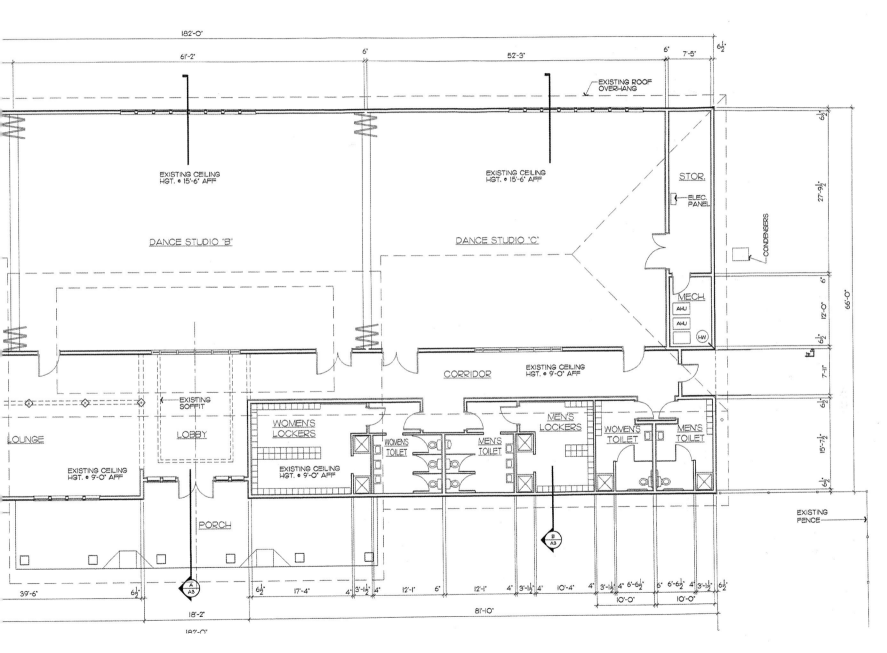

School of the Arts

The Museum's School of the Arts was established in the mid-2000s at the Swyer Studios, and reinvented in 2008 under the direction of Raul P. Martinez to accommodate a distinctly larger scope of classes and students. Occupying the Studios all twelve months of the year, the evolution of the number of students, the quantity of classes offered, and the growth of its reputation has been exponential in the last decade. The School of the Arts promotes inclusivity within a non-pressure environment, and offers a robust scholarship program based on financial need, commitment, and ability through which no child is ever turned away. Scholarships awarded range from ten percent to one hundred percent of tuition costs. An exceptional faculty, representing a wide breadth of performance and teaching experience, trains students across generations and levels, including those with professional aspirations. Today enrollments total more than four hundred for engagement in multiple styles of dance, with ballet remaining its strength. A summer ballet intensive led by members of PHILADANCO and NYCB is also offered. With the Riggi Theater as the Museum's newest resource, music and theater arts instruction are an emerging aspect of the School of the Arts curriculum.

FACING PAGE:
School of the Arts modern dance class performing *Under Water* (2016), choreography by Laurie Zabele Cawley, at the showcase performance, 2016.

LEFT:
School of the Arts instructor Cristiane Santos teaching ballet class.

Performance opportunities for students include *The Nutcracker, Act II, Kingdom of the Sweets* and the annual spring showcase. Since 2008, acclaimed fashion and costume designer Kim Vanyo of Khymanyo Studio has been instrumental in developing the distinct aesthetic of the School from the conservatory-style tunics worn in class to the original, handmade costumes she has created for each of the School's performances such as *Paquita, La Bayadère, Don Quixote, La Vivandière*, and *La Fille mal gardée*, in addition to several modern dance works.

CLOCKWISE FROM BOTTOM LEFT:
Kim Vanyo in a costume fitting for *Don Quixote*.

School of the Arts ballet class.

Students in the School of the Arts summer intensive.

Instructor Joan K. Anderson teaching a modern dance class.

FACING PAGE, PERFORMANCES FROM THE ANNUAL SHOWCASE, CLOCKWISE FROM TOP LEFT:
"Golden Idol" from *La Bayadère*, belly dance, *Paquita, I See Fire*, backstage before *The Sleeping Beauty*, Irish Step, and *Friend's Waltz*.

FACING PAGE CLOCKWISE FROM TOP LEFT:
Scenes from the annual performance of *The Nutcracker*: Angels, Snow Pas de Deux, Mother Ginger, Clara and the Prince, Sugarplum Fairy and her Cavalier with guest artist Isaac Akiba, soloist from the Boston Ballet.

CLOCKWISE FROM TOP LEFT:
Scenes from the annual performance of *The Nutcracker*: Chinese, Spanish, costume designer Kim Vanyo with Museum and School of the Arts director Raul P. Martinez as Mother Ginger, Arabian, and Waltz of the Flowers.

Residencies

The NYSSSA Schools of Ballet and Dance have been the longest-running annual auditions and residencies held at the Studios, beginning when the facility opened in the summer of 1992. The School of Ballet selects sixty students from across New York State to participate in this four-week intensive each July in which participants train daily at the Studios with NYCB dancers and faculty from the School of American Ballet, and attend performances at SPAC in the evenings. School of Ballet artistic directors have included principal dancers Heather Watts, Damian Woetzel, Jenifer Ringer, and Daniel Ulbricht.

FACING PAGE:
Students from NYSSSA's School of Dance.

LEFT:
Robert Battle with Julie Adams Strandberg and Carolyn Adams, artistic directors of NYSSSA's School of Dance.

The School of Dance was founded in 1988 by Carolyn Adams, a former Paul Taylor Dance Company member, who continues to co-direct the program with her sister, the renowned dance artist and educator Julie Adams Strandberg. This four-week intensive each August is a collaboration between the New York State Education Department and the American Dance Legacy Initiative in which thirty students of modern dance are introduced to the works of American dance masters through the Repertory Etudes program. Guest teachers have included Donald McKayle, Sophie Maslow, Ruth Andrien, Ethel Winter, David Parsons, and Robert Battle.[11] Another longstanding student residency at the Swyer Studios is the Saratoga Summer Dance Intensive, founded by Roberto Muñoz and Melinda Roy.

LEFT TO RIGHT:
Students in NYSSSA's School of Dance.

FACING PAGE:
Donald McKayle teaching in NYSSSA's School of Dance.

FACING PAGE:
Students from the Saratoga Summer Dance Intensive.

CLOCKWISE FROM TOP LEFT:
Roberto Muñoz and students in the Saratoga Summer Dance Intensive.

Professional artist residencies at the Studios have included but have not been limited to dance. The first significant example was the Dance Theatre of Harlem's three-week residency in 2000 through the company's Dancing Through Barriers educational outreach program, followed by troupes such as Risa Jaroslow and Dancers, LEIMAY, and Annabella Gonzalez Dance Theater. Examples outside of dance include the Labyrinth Theater Company's two-week residency through Saratoga Stages in 2002.[12] Karole Armitage is one of several choreographer-directors who have utilized the Studios to create new work. In 2015 she choreographed the opera *Dido and Aeneas* on site, a production she directed for Opera Saratoga that was performed in the Museum's courtyard. She returned the following year to choreograph her Opera Saratoga production of *The Witches of Venice*.

Opera Saratoga's 2015 production of *Dido and Aeneas*, directed and choreographed by Karole Armitage, performed in the courtyard of the Museum.

Master Classes and Lecture-Demonstrations

A multitude of master classes and lecture-demonstrations representing a broad spectrum of the art form have been offered at the Studios since 1992. While many of these events have been organized in conjunction with Museum exhibitions and Hall of Fame inductions, others have been realized through residencies or performances at regional arts venues such as SPAC, Skidmore College, The Egg, and Jacob's Pillow. World-renowned companies from the National Ballet of China and the Bolshoi Ballet to Alvin Ailey American Dance Theater and Martha Graham Dance Company have taught in the Studios, in addition to a host of celebrated dancer-choreographers from Arthur Mitchell and Justin Peck to Bill T. Jones and David Parsons. Master classes outside of ballet and modern dance have featured, for example, tap dance with Brenda Buffalino and Jason Samuels Smith, Kathak with Shila Mehta, and singing, dancing, and acting with Ben Vereen. The vast range of lecture-demonstrations presented include Jacob's Pillow's Men Dancers, Ballet Boyz, Ellen Sinopoli Dance Company, Miami City Ballet, Ronald K. Brown and Evidence, The Limón Dance Company, PHILADANCO, and Savion Glover.

FACING PAGE, LEFT TO RIGHT:
Arthur Mitchell teaching a master class in the Studios, 2014.

Arthur Mitchell with costume designer Kim Vanyo, 2014.

LEFT:
Former NYCB principal dancer and founder of Dance Theatre of Harlem Arthur Mitchell.

FACING PAGE:
Students in a master class taught by Bill T. Jones, 2010.

CLOCKWISE FROM TOP LEFT:
Lecture-demonstration given by Bill T. Jones, 2010.

Bill T. Jones photographed at the Museum.

Bill T. Jones with SPAC's former president and executive director Marcia White.

FACING PAGE AND THIS PAGE:
Master class with Brian Simerson of MOMIX, 2014.

ABOVE:
Master class with tap artist Jason Samuels Smith, 2010.

RIGHT:
Master class with Alexander Vetrov from the Bolshoi Ballet, 2014.

FACING PAGE LEFT AND RIGHT:
Alvin Ailey master class with Dwight Rhoden and Renee Robinson in the Studios, June 11, 1992.

FACING PAGE:
Carla Maxwell, legacy director of José Limón Dance Company, leading a master class, May 10, 2017.

THIS PAGE:
José Limón Dance Company master class in the Studios with Carla Maxwell in 2010, 2011 and 2017.

213

Programming and Special Events

Collaborative programming and special events further distinguish the Studios as a premier venue for comprehensive arts education in the region. Museum exhibitions such as *Postage Paid*, *125 Years of Tango*, and *The Dancing Athlete* have most recently inspired dance education programming and outreach in the Studios. For the past several years, the Museum has also conceived and sponsored specialized dance days such as national, international, multicultural, and family. Annual events such as Dancer Health Day and Black History Month celebrations further explored dance within multiple contexts. A longstanding partnership with the Dance Alliance has brought not only emerging choreographers to the Studios but masterclasses and annual programming such as the Dance+ Festival. Inspired by the Hall of Fame, Dance+ is now in its twenty-seventh year. Dancing Through Time, a Dance Alliance program for students aged fifty-five and older, was also inspired by the Hall of Fame and featured visionary choreographers and directors such as Doug Varone as guest artists.[13]

FACING PAGE:
The Adirondack Thunder, a professional hockey team in the East Coast Hockey League (ECHL), taking a dance class at the Studios, November 30, 2016.

LEFT:
Students in a Broadway jazz class taught by Janet Murphy (not pictured) as part of the Dance+23 Festival, April 14, 2013.

LEFT, CLOCKWISE FROM TOP LEFT:
The Adirondack Thunder ECHL team toured *The Dancing Athlete* exhibition and took a dance class taught by Johnny Martinez of Tango Fusion, November 30, 2016.

TOP RIGHT:
The Saratoga Springs freshman baseball team taking a dance class taught by Anny DeGange Holgate, May 5, 2016.

FACING PAGE, CLOCKWISE FROM TOP LEFT:
Mary DiSanto-Rose (kneeling at center, with program director Marilyn Rothstein standing behind her) leading a Dancing Through Time Isadora Duncan class, circa 2011.

Mary Jane Dyke in the Dancing Through Time Isadora Duncan class, circa 2011.

Robert Maiorano teaching in the Dancing Through Time program.

Students in a modern dance class taught by Matt Pardo (not pictured) as part of the Dance+23 Festival, April 14, 2013.

Students in a contemporary dance class taught by André Robles as part of the Dance+23 Festival, April 14, 2013.

CLOCKWISE FROM TOP LEFT:
Clifford Oliver performing during
Black History Month at the Museum,
February 2015.

Yonka Beckham teaching dance class in
the Studios during Black History Month,
February 2013.

The Heavenly Echoes gospel acapella
group from Mount Olivet Baptist Church
performing for Black History Month,
February 2013.

Anna Blanton, Stephen Tyson, Dora Lee
Stanley, and Neil de Grasse Tyson during
Black History Month, February 2013.

Artist Francelise Dawkins,
Black History Month, February 2013.

FACING PAGE:
Ben Vereen performing during
Black History Month, 2012.

THIS PAGE:
Dancer Health Days, 2012 and 2013.

FACING PAGE:
Participants in the 2012 Dancer Health Day included from left, Julia Erickson, principal dancer with Pittsburgh Ballet Theater; Eliza Minden, head of design at Gaynor Minden; Dr. Linda Hamilton, wellness consultant for NYCB; Meghan Del Prete, owner of Reform: A True Pilates Studio; and Kim Teter, physical therapist and former American Ballet Theatre dancer.

FACING PAGE, CLOCKWISE FROM TOP LEFT:
Ricardo Sopin and Iraida Volodina performing during National Dance Day, 2012.

Yonka Beckham teaching dance class during National Dance Day, 2012.

The Puppet People performed *The Firebird* in the Studios, followed by a puppet-making workshop, 2013.

Albany Symphony Orchestra annual Tiny Tots concert, 2017.

TOP LEFT AND RIGHT:
India Day, 2010.

BOTTOM LEFT AND RIGHT:
Africa Day, 2011.

Since its inception, the Museum has hosted compelling events that have directly impacted, influenced, and raised awareness for the vastly diverse community that comprises dance. In 1995, *Dances from the Heart* was presented in the Studios, a dance concert and benefit for Dancers Responding to AIDS. This vital not-for-profit organization has provided support to members of the dance industry living with HIV/AIDS for more than twenty-five years. Artists such as Albert Evans, Judith Fugate, and Lourdes Lopez of NYCB; Virginia Johnson, Kellye Gordon, and Donald Williams of Dance Theatre of Harlem; and Robert Battle of the Parsons Dance Company performed the outstanding program. More recently, performances by Figures in Flight: Released and a documentary film screening of *Reflections of Our Lives Through Dance* highlighted the groundbreaking Figures in Flight 5 modern dance program at the Woodburne Correctional Facility.[14]

CLOCKWISE FROM TOP RIGHT:
Figures in Flight: Released performing in the Studios, 2013.

Figures in Flight: Released, director and soloist, Andre Noel, performing in the Studios, 2012.

Program from *Dances from the Heart*, a dance concert and benefit for Dancers Responding to AIDS, July 10, 1995.

FACING PAGE:
Figures in Flight: Released performing in the Studios, 2013.

Galas

For the past thirty years, the Museum's highly anticipated gala each August has remained its largest annual fundraiser. *An Evening in Old Saratoga*, the inaugural gala in the 1986 preview season, served to introduce the Museum to local philanthropists but also to the distinct assemblage of horse owners, breeders, socialites, and celebrities that has converged on the city during the August racing season for generations.[15] In 1984, Cornelius Vanderbilt Whitney described August in Saratoga Springs as "the most important place to be in the United States, for the thoroughbreds, the performing arts and because friends come from everywhere to be here."[16] From its earliest days, Mr. and Mrs. Whitney propelled the Museum to the forefront of the Saratoga social season by holding the Museum gala on the day of the historic Whitney Stakes at the Saratoga Race Course and the night after the legendary Whitney gala, a keystone of the summer party circuit.

The 1987 grand opening season gala quite aptly adopted the theme of *A Midsummer Night's Dream*. The event honored former Kentucky governor John Y. Brown and his wife Phyllis George Brown as well as NYCB's Peter Martins. Nearly six hundred guests, including Liza Minnelli who was in town to perform at SPAC, were welcomed in a vast tent positioned behind the Museum, splendidly decorated with foliage, fairies, butterflies, and the like.[17] The event raised more than $100,000 and was considered such a success that the subsequent two galas celebrated this same theme.

FACING PAGE:
Tents erected behind the Museum for the 1987 gala, *A Midsummer Night's Dream*, August 8, 1987.

ABOVE:
Gary Collins, Marylou Whitney, Phyllis George Brown, and Mary Ann Mobley at the brunch the day after *A Midsummer Night's Dream* gala, August 9, 1987.

227

The first several galas were designed to be national in reach, with gala chairs and committees totaling over two hundred well-connected individuals from a host of local philanthropists and arts patrons to socialites such as C. Z. Guest and celebrities such as Merv Griffin, thoroughbred owners such as Henryk de Kwiatkowski and notable friends such as publisher and founder of the International Tennis Hall of Fame James Van Alen. Thoroughbred owners Sheryl and Barry Schwartz were steadfast supporters of the Museum and chaired a number of galas beginning in the late 1980s.[18] All of the galas were held in tents on the property until the Swyer Studios were built in 1992, at which point, the event was moved to this indoor space. For four years during the 1990s, in lieu of the Museum hosting its own gala, the annual Whitney gala at the Canfield Casino exclusively benefited the Museum.[19]

RIGHT:
Program for the 1989 gala, *A Midsummer's Night Dream*, cover photograph by Bruce Weber, August 5, 1989.

FACING PAGE, CLOCKWISE FROM TOP LEFT:
Marylou Whitney, former Kentucky governor John Y. Brown, Phyllis George Brown, and Lewis A. Swyer at the August 8, 1987 gala that honored Governor Brown.

Marylou Whitney's 1954 MG TF Roadster, a raffle item at the 1988 gala, August 6, 1988.

Ginger Rogers at the Museum's preview season gala, *An Evening in Old Saratoga*, August 2, 1986.

Mr. and Mrs. Walter Cronkite at the 1986 gala.

Robin Leach and Judith Ledford at Marylou Whitney's *Saratoga Trunk* gala at the Canfield Casino that benefited the Museum, August 3, 1990.

Marylou Whitney and Gary Collins at the August 5, 1989 gala.

Philanthropist and socialite Mollie Wilmot, who divided her time between homes in Manhattan, Palm Beach, and Saratoga Springs, also organized a series of memorable galas, including the 1994 *Homage to Nureyev*. Honoring both world-renowned dancer Rudolf Nureyev and his equine namesake, one of the most prolific and successful sires of his time, Wilmot chose a Moroccan theme based on Nureyev's signature work, *La Bayadère*.[20] Created by Palm Beach designer Scott Snyder, the Swyer Studios were transformed into a festival tent of kings. Under a canopy of gold lamé, walls were paneled in green, red, and gold, Oriental rugs were strewn with rose petals, and brass lanterns abounded. Tables were dressed with hand-loomed tapestries, fruit, and gold place settings, flatware, and chairs. Of the event Marylou Whitney remarked, "I've been to all the parties in the world and this is the most magnificent. It was like walking into a fantasy world."[21] This particular gala was so highly anticipated that even Bill Cunningham from *The New York Times* made the three-hour trip north to document it.[22]

FACING PAGE, LEFT TO RIGHT:
Program for the *Can Can* gala, August 3, 1991.

Marylou Whitney and Chelsea Myers at the 1991 *Can Can* gala.

CLOCKWISE FROM TOP LEFT:
Homage to Nureyev table-setting featuring hand-loomed tapestries, fruit, and gold place settings, flatware, and chairs.

Gala chair Mollie Wilmot and Charles Washburn at the August 6, 1994 *Homage to Nureyev* gala.

Ornate wall decorations and canopies transformed the Swyer Studios into a festival tent of kings.

CLOCKWISE FROM TOP LEFT:
Ron and Michele Riggi with Marylou Whitney and John Hendrickson at the *Cirque de Danse* gala, August 2, 2008.

Ann-Margret at the *Silver Anniversary* gala, August 6, 2011.

Neil and Jane Golub at the *¡Tango!* gala, August 8, 2015.

FACING PAGE:
Iraida Volodina and a performer from World Gate Entertainment at the *¡Tango!* gala, August 8, 2015.

In recent years, annual Hall of Fame inductions have been integrated into the gala program, becoming a centerpiece of the evening. Live dance performance has also become a critical aspect of the event, a purposeful reflection of the mission of the Museum to promote and foster a greater understanding and appreciation of the art form. Unforgettable gala performances have been given by a wide range of artists including Marge Champion and Donald Saddler, Ben Vereen, American Ballet Theatre, MOMIX, Alvin Ailey American Dance Theater, and Tommy Tune.[23] Some of the most memorable galas of late include *Dancers in Film* (2014) attended by Hall of Fame inductee Jacques d'Amboise and Mariano Rivera of the New York Yankees serving as honorary chair, *¡Tango!* (2015) at which Mark Morris accepted his Hall of Fame induction, and *The Dancing Athlete* (2016) which hosted Hall of Fame inductee Patricia Wilde and Savion Glover who accepted the induction award of Gregory Hines on behalf of the Hines family.[24] Through this event, the Museum continues to raise more than thirty percent of its operating budget each year.

LEFT TO RIGHT:
Christine Shevchenko and Gray Davis of American Ballet Theatre performing at the *Silver Anniversary* gala, August 6, 2011.

Tommy Tune performing at the *Gala on Broadway*, August 1, 2009.

FACING PAGE:
Nicole Loizides and Steven Ezra of MOMIX performing *Millenium Skiva* (1999), choreography by Moses Pendleton, at the *Silver Anniversary* gala, August 6, 2011.

CHAPTER FIVE

Timeline

The fascinating history of the Museum is clearly expressed through its considerable roster of exhibitions and programming, the evolution of the Hall of Fame, and the growth of the collection. The essence of the Museum is a distinct reflection of those who have cared deeply and resolutely about its development and its success over the course of three decades, from the founders to the volunteers and beyond. A vital tradition of collaboration and community has endured and flourished. The principles and singular spirit with which the National Museum of Dance and Hall of Fame was established thirty years ago remain fundamental to its mission as they inform all facets of this unique cultural institution and propel it toward the future.

FACING PAGE:
Vintage postcard, view of the pergola and grounds, circa 1920s.

1986

CLOCKWISE FROM TOP LEFT:
Model and concept drawing for the Museum, displayed at the May 12, 1986 press conference.

Mrs. John A. Morris, Marylou Whitney, and Kitty Carlisle Hart at the June 5, 1986 Grand Carriage Parade in Manhattan.

The Museum's first director Alison Moore and Marylou Whitney at the gala, *An Evening in Old Saratoga*, August 2, 1986.

Repeated Phrase (1981) by Dana Reitz, from Quintet Project #1, charcoal on paper, displayed in the exhibition *Tracking, Tracing, Marking, Pacing*.

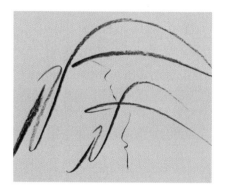

Exhibitions:

Made in America: Modern Dance Then and Now

Tracking, Tracing, Marking, Pacing

Dressing the Ballet: Costumes from America's Most Celebrated Companies

The National Museum of Dance: Development of a Dream

Gala:

An Evening in Old Saratoga

Notable:

Alison Moore was appointed director.

1987

CLOCKWISE FROM TOP LEFT:

William and Susan Dake at the brunch the day after *A Midsummer Night's Dream* gala, August 9, 1987.

Kay Bardsley (right) accepted the Hall of Fame award for Isadora Duncan.

The first Hall of Fame brochure created by the Museum.

Costumes from the original Broadway production of *A Chorus Line*, displayed in the exhibition *Shall We Dance? Costumes from Broadway and Hollywood*.

Exhibitions:

Shall We Dance? Costumes from Broadway and Hollywood

Portraiture in Dance: Photographs by Kenn Duncan

Shaping the American Dance Dream: The Founders

Hall of Fame Inductees:

Fred Astaire

George Balanchine

Agnes de Mille

Isadora Duncan

Katherine Dunham

Martha Graham

Doris Humphrey

Lincoln Kirstein

Catherine Littlefield

Bill "Bojangles" Robinson

Ruth St. Denis

Ted Shawn

Charles Weidman

Gala:

A Midsummer Night's Dream

1988

NATIONAL MUSEUM OF DANCE

1988 Season

CLOCKWISE FROM TOP LEFT:

Volunteers at the brunch the day after *A Midsummer Night's Dream* gala, August 7, 1988.

Marylou Whitney at the brunch in front of her 1954 MG TF Roadster, a gala raffle item, August 7, 1988.

The 1988 season brochure.

Museum visitors viewing *The Fugitive Gesture: Masterpieces of Dance Photography 1849 to the Present*.

Exhibitions:

The Fugitive Gesture: Masterpieces of Dance Photography 1849 to the Present

Ballet for a City and a Nation: Forty Years of the New York City Ballet

Shaping the American Dance Dream: The Founders

Hall of Fame Inductees:

Busby Berkeley

Lucia Chase

Hanya Holm

John Martin

Antony Tudor

Gala:

A Midsummer Night's Dream

Notable:

The Museum and the Lewis A. Swyer Company were honored by the Preservation League of New York State with the Adaptive Use Award for the preservation and reuse of the historic Washington Baths.

1989

CLOCKWISE FROM TOP LEFT:
The Three Graces, lithograph by Nathaniel Currier, N.Y., (416), displayed in the exhibition *Great Ballet Prints of the Romantic Era*.

Founding board member Nancy Norman Lassalle and artist Hope Hawthorne holding the stained glass Hall of Fame award designed and made by Hawthorne.

Judith Brown's *Blithe Spirits*, displayed on the lawn of the Museum as part of the exhibition *Figures in Motion*.

Patricia and William F. Snyder at *A Midsummer Night's Dream* gala, August 5, 1989.

Maria Calegari accepting the Hall of Fame award for Jerome Robbins, August 6, 1989.

Exhibitions:

Black Dance in Photographs

Great Ballet Prints of the Romantic Era

The Fugitive Gesture: Masterpieces of Dance Photography 1849 to the Present

Ballet for a City and a Nation: Forty Years of the New York City Ballet

Shaping the American Dance Dream

Figures in Motion—outdoor exhibition of Judith Brown's welded steel sculpture

Hall of Fame Inductee:

Jerome Robbins

Gala:

A Midsummer Night's Dream

Notable:

The Sales Gallery opened in the southeast gallery featuring paintings and sculpture by Judith Brown.

1990

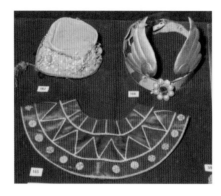
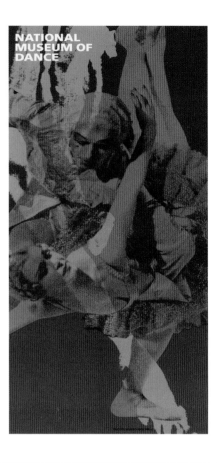

CLOCKWISE FROM TOP LEFT:

Judith Brown's *Athena* was a gift from Anne Swyer.

Museum administrator Sharon Walsh and a guest from Leningrad at the opening of *100 Years of Russian Ballet: 1830-1930*.

The Museum's 1990 season brochure.

Costume pieces from *100 Years of Russian Ballet: 1830-1930*.

Exhibitions:
100 Years of Russian Ballet: 1830–1930

Les Ballets 1933

Shaping the American Dance Dream

Hall of Fame Inductee:
none

Gala:
The *Saratoga Trunk* gala hosted by Marylou Whitney at the Canfield Casino benefited the National Museum of Dance

Notable:
The Museum became a program of SPAC.

Athena by Judith Brown was permanently installed in the front circle of the Museum, a gift from Anne Swyer.

The Sales Gallery featured photographs by Paul Kolnik.

1991

CLOCKWISE FROM TOP LEFT:

Barbara Morgan at the opening of the exhibition *Barbara Morgan: Prints, Drawings, Watercolors, and Photographs*, May 17, 1991.

A Museum visitor in front of the set for Ted Shawn's *Cosmic Dance of Siva* (1926), displayed in the exhibition *Ted Shawn: A Centennial Tribute to the Father of American Dance.*

Exhibitions:

Ted Shawn: A Centennial Tribute to the Father of American Dance

Rites of Passage: 25 Years of the School of American Ballet Workshop Performances

Barbara Morgan: Prints, Drawings, Watercolors, and Photographs

Shaping the American Dance Dream

Hall of Fame Inductee:

Gala:

Can Can

Notable:

Joanne Allison was appointed director.

The Sales Gallery featured *Portraits of the Ballerina* by Alan Kluckow.

1992

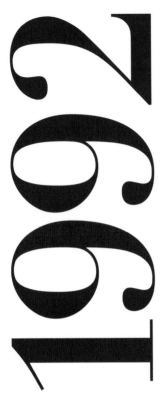

NATIONAL MUSEUM OF DANCE

CLOCKWISE FROM TOP LEFT:
Carol, Edward, and Anne Swyer at Alvin Ailey's induction into the Hall of Fame, June 11, 1992.

Guests at the gala, *An Evening of Stardust Memories*, July 25, 1992.

Gala raffle ticket.

The Museum's booklet for the Hall of Fame.

A view of the exhibition *Body and Soul: The Alvin Ailey American Dance Theater*.

Exhibitions:

Body and Soul: The Alvin Ailey American Dance Theater

The Still Point: Images from Dancers' Bodies: Original Drawings by Betti Franceschi

Ted Shawn: A Centennial Tribute to the Father of American Dance

Hall of Fame Inductee:

Alvin Ailey

Gala:

An Evening of Stardust Memories

Notable:

The Lewis A. Swyer School for the Performing Arts opened.

The Museum received $100,000 from the estate of Hanya Holm.

The Mr. and Mrs. Cornelius Vanderbilt Whitney Hall of Fame was renovated and reopened.

1993

Rhapsody in Blue

CLOCKWISE FROM TOP LEFT:
Mark Morris at Merce Cunningham's Hall of Fame induction, June 20, 1993.

Stage costume worn by M.C. Hammer. Gift of an anonymous donor.

Rhapsody in Blue gala program.

Joan Rivers at the *Rhapsody in Blue* gala, August 7, 1993.

Museum visitors viewing a video in the Merce Cunningham Hall of Fame installation.

Exhibitions:
*Balanchine:
A Celebration of His Work*

Merce Cunningham: Points in Time

Hall of Fame Inductee:
Merce Cunningham

Gala:
Rhapsody in Blue

1994

Homage to Nureyev

NATIONAL MUSEUM OF DANCE
1994 GALA PROGRAM

NATIONAL MUSEUM OF DANCE

1994 SEASON

National Museum of Dance
99 South Broadway
Saratoga Springs, NY 12866
518-584-2225
a program of the
Saratoga Performing Arts Center

CLOCKWISE FROM TOP LEFT:
Marylou Whitney and Mollie Wilmot at the *Homage to Nureyev* gala, August 6, 1994.

Program for the *Homage to Nureyev* gala.

The Museum's 1994 season brochure.

A view of the installation in progress for the exhibition *Balanchine: A Celebration of His Work*.

Exhibitions:
Bronislava Nijinska: Classic on the Edge

Balanchine: A Celebration of His Work

Hall of Fame Inductee:
Bronislava Nijinska

Gala:
Homage to Nureyev

Notable:
The Sales Gallery featured *Exposed: The Dancer Backstage*, photographs by Michele Wambaugh.

1995

CLOCKWISE FROM TOP LEFT:
Paul Taylor at his Hall of Fame induction, May 27, 1995.

Edward Swyer (far left) and the Museum's second director Joanne Allison (far right) at the opening of the exhibition *Paul Taylor: In His Own Words*.

Save the Date for the *Homage to Fred Astaire* gala.

Mollie Wilmot with Shaun O'Brien (far right) at the *Homage to Fred Astaire* gala, August 5, 1995.

Maria Tallchief at the opening of the exhibition *Firebird and the New York City Ballet 1949-1995*, July 20, 1995.

Exhibitions:
Firebird and the New York City Ballet 1949–1995

Paul Taylor: In His Own Words

Francisco Moncion: A Life in Dance and Art

Hall of Fame Inductee:
Paul Taylor

Gala:
Homage to Fred Astaire

1996

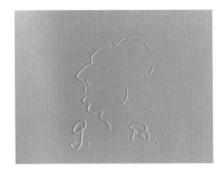

CLOCKWISE FROM TOP LEFT:
Program for the *Homage to George Balanchine* gala.

Set design by Marc Chagall for *Firebird* (1949), choreography by George Balanchine and Jerome Robbins, original sets designed by Marc Chagall and executed under the supervision of Volodia Odinokov, ©The George Balanchine Trust, displayed in the exhibition *Firebird and the New York City Ballet 1949-1995*.

Headpiece from *Firebird* (1949), choreography by George Balanchine and Jerome Robbins, original costumes designed by Marc Chagall and executed by Karinska, Firebird costume supervised by Dain Marcus, ©The George Balanchine Trust. Gift of NYCB.

Program director Toni Smith.

Exhibitions:
Paul Sanasardo in Max Waldman's View

Firebird and the New York City Ballet 1949–1995

Hall of Fame Inductee:
none

Gala:
Homage to George Balanchine

Notable:
Toni Smith was appointed program director.

1997

CLOCKWISE FROM TOP LEFT:
Fury Observed from the exhibition *Visible Breath: Images of Dance*–photographs by William R. Boorstein, ©1994 William Boorstein/Boorstein.com.

Invitation to the Hall of Fame induction of José Limón, July 13, 1997.

Pauline Koner speaking at the Hall of Fame induction of José Limón.

Invitation to the *Silver Buck* Whitney gala that benefited the Museum, August 1, 1997

Exhibitions:
The Dance Heroes of José Limón

Visible Breath: Images of Dance–
photographs by William R. Boorstein

Hall of Fame Inductee:
José Limón

Gala:
The *Silver Buck* gala hosted by Marylou Whitney at the Canfield Casino benefited the National Museum of Dance

Notable:
Maurice O'Connell was appointed operations manager.

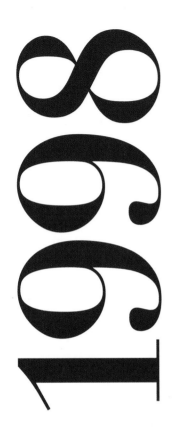

1998

masks stagecraft
costumes
from her world of dance & myth

jean erdman

[May 1998 through April 1999]

[National Museum of Dance]

CLOCKWISE FROM TOP LEFT:

Mary Ann Mobley, Marylou Whitney, and John Hendrickson at *The Phantom of the Opera* Whitney gala that benefited the Museum.

Anna Sokolow (in black dress) with Norton Owen (far right) at her Hall of Fame induction, July 19, 1998.

Brochure for the exhibition *Jean Erdman: Masks, Costumes, and Stagecraft from her World of Dance and Myth*.

Invitation to the Hall of Fame induction of Anna Sokolow.

Exhibitions:

Anna Sokolow: The Rebellious Spirit

Jean Erdman: Masks, Costumes, and Stagecraft from her World of Dance and Myth

Dancers of Limón: Photographs by Susan Rubin

Hall of Fame Inductee:

Anna Sokolow

Gala:

The Phantom of the Opera gala hosted by Marylou Whitney at the Canfield Casino benefited the National Museum of Dance

1999

CLOCKWISE FROM TOP LEFT:

Merrill Ashley with students from NYSSSA's School of Ballet at the reception and work-in-progress preview of the documentary about Ashley, *The Dance Goodbye* (2014), July 16, 1999.

Costumes from *Ballet Imperial* (Ballet Caravan premiere 1941, NYCB premiere 1964), choreography by George Balanchine, costume by Rouben Ter-Arutunian, on display in the exhibition *New York City Ballet: Our Time in Saratoga Springs*, ©The George Balanchine Trust.

A view of the exhibition *New York City Ballet: Our Time in Saratoga Springs*.

Invitation to the *Showboat* Whitney gala that benefited the Museum, August 6, 1999.

Exhibitions:

Arthur Mitchell: From Harlem with Love

New York City Ballet: Our Time in Saratoga Springs

The Energy of Dance: Michael Philip Manheim Photography

Hall of Fame Inductees:

Arthur Mitchell

Barbara Karinska

Gala:

The *Showboat* gala hosted by Mary-lou Whitney at the Canfield Casino benefited the National Museum of Dance

Notable:

Siobhan Dunham was appointed interim artistic director.

An Interactive Children's Room was created in the southwest gallery.

2000

CLOCKWISE FROM TOP LEFT:

Former board president Heather Mabee at the *Gene Kelly Singin' the Rain* gala, July 28, 2000.

Dr. Richard Dunham and interim artistic director Siobhan Dunham at the gala.

Mark Baker ringing the dinner bell at the gala.

Marylou Whitney with Barbara Ecker at the *Gene Kelly Singin' in the Rain* gala.

Gala invitation.

Exhibitions:

An American Mosaic:
Dance Photos by Steven Caras

New York City Ballet:
Our Time in Saratoga Springs

The Energy of Dance:
Michael Philip Manheim Photography

Hall of Fame Inductees:

Trisha Brown

Robert Joffrey

Alwin Nikolais

Gala:

Gene Kelly Singin' in the Rain

2001

CLOCKWISE FROM TOP LEFT:

Savion Glover and Deirdre Dunham, daughter of interim artistic director Siobhan Dunham, at the Hall of Fame induction of Fayard and Harold Nicholas, August 5, 2001.

A student from the School of American Ballet viewing the exhibition, *An American Mosaic: Dance Photos by Steven Caras*. Gift of Steven Caras, 2017, ©Steven Caras, all rights reserved.

Fayard Nicholas at his Hall of Fame induction.

Invitation to *The Nicholas Brothers That's Dancing!* gala, August 4, 2001.

That's Dancing!

Exhibitions:

*Spaces of the Mind:
Isamu Noguchi's Dance Designs*

*The Fugitive Gesture:
Masterpieces of Dance Photography
1849 to the Present*–a reprise of the
1988 exhibition

*An American Mosaic:
Dance Photos by Steven Caras*

Hall of Fame Inductees:

Fayard and Harold Nicholas

Gala:

*The Nicholas Brothers That's
Dancing!*

2002

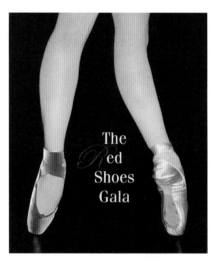

CLOCKWISE FROM TOP LEFT:
Invitation to the Hall of Fame induction of Edwin Denby and Léonide Massine, August 4, 2002.

Longtime volunteer Mary Anne Fantauzzi at *The Red Shoes* gala, August 3, 2002.

Artistic director Jacques Burgering, future director Donna Skiff, and operations manager Maurice O'Connell at the gala.

Invitation to *The Red Shoes* gala.

Exhibitions:

Classic Black

The Art of Light-The Art of Dance–photographs by Lawrence White

Visions of Dance–photographs by David Michalek

Spaces of the Mind: Isamu Noguchi's Dance Designs

The Fugitive Gesture: Masterpieces of Dance Photography 1849 to the Present–a reprise of the 1988 exhibition

Hall of Fame Inductees:

Léonide Massine

Edwin Orr Denby

Gala:

The Red Shoes

Notable:

Jacques Burgering was appointed artistic director.

2003

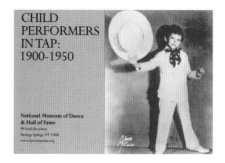

CLOCKWISE FROM TOP LEFT:

Invitation to the opening of *Child Performers in Tap: 1900-1950.*

A photograph of James, Gene, and Fred Kelly displayed in the exhibition *Child Performers in Tap: 1900-1950.*

The Museum's 2003 season brochure.

Invitation to the *On the Town* gala, August 2, 2003.

Exhibitions:
Child Performers in Tap: 1900–1950

The Art of Light-The Art of Dance—photographs by Lawrence White

Hall of Fame Inductee:
none

Gala:
On the Town

Notable:
The Museum declared 2003 as the Year of Tap.

2004

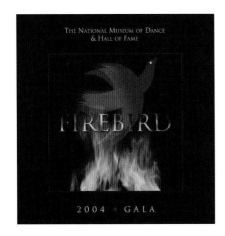

CLOCKWISE FROM TOP LEFT:

Invitation to the *Firebird* gala, August 7, 2004.

Banner for the exhibition *30 Years of Ballet Barbie Dolls: A Child's Introduction to Story Ballets*.

A view of *30 Years of Ballet Barbie Dolls: A Child's Introduction to Story Ballets*.

Artist Bogusław Lustyk who created the outdoor exhibition *Dance Garden*.

Exhibition brochure for *The Enduring Legacy of George Balanchine*. BALANCHINE is a Trademark of The George Balanchine Trust.

Exhibitions:

Saratoga Remembers Balanchine

The Enduring Legacy of George Balanchine

Golden Land/Golden Dreams: Images of Sacred Temple Dances and Dancers from the Kingdom of Cambodia–photographs by Mark Sadan

30 Years of Ballet Barbie Dolls: A Child's Introduction to Story Ballets

Child Performers in Tap: 1900-1950

Dance Garden–Bogusław Lustyk–outdoor exhibition

Hall of Fame Inductee:

Igor Stravinsky

Dancer Hall of Fame Inductees:

Edward Villella

Suzanne Farrell

Marge Champion

Gala:

Firebird

Notable:

Garrett Smith was appointed director.

Interpretations of Degas' Dancers, an exhibition of artwork created by local elementary school students was on display.

2005

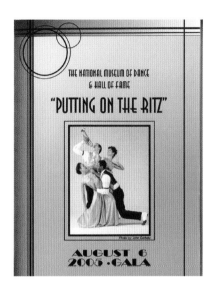

CLOCKWISE FROM TOP LEFT:

Works of art from the children's workshop Dance and Draw.

Participants dancing around a May pole in the children's program Story, Dance, and Play.

A view of the exhibition *Dancing Rebels: The New Dance Group.*

Invitation to the *Putting on the Ritz* gala.

Exhibitions:

Dancing Rebels:
The New Dance Group

Golden Land/Golden Dreams:
Images of Sacred Temple Dances and
Dancers from the Kingdom of Cam-
bodia–photographs by Mark Sadan

Child Performers in Tap: 1900–1950

Dance Through the Eyes
of World Youth

Hall of Fame Inductee:

Gala:

Putting on the Ritz

Notable:

Beth Hartle was appointed artistic director.

2006

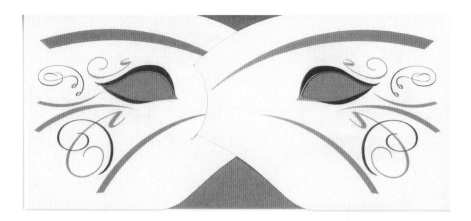

CLOCKWISE FROM TOP LEFT:

Guests at the *Masquerade* gala, August 5, 2006.

Invitation to the *Masquerade* gala.

A view of the exhibition *Dance of the Iroquois*.

Invitation to the opening of *Eleanor Rigby's Resurrection*, August 11, 2006.

Exhibitions:

Dance of the Iroquois

Memoirs of a Lake George Showboat Performer: Edith Tulloch de Polac

Dancing Rebels:
The New Dance Group

Dance Across New York

The Young Dancer:
Photography by Mark Sadan

Eleanor Rigby's Resurrection:
Images Inspired by Music's Icons—
photographs by Mark Andrew of choreography by Beth Hartle

Art in the Foyer:

Dance Photography:
On the Edge—Lawrence White

Dance: East Meets West—*20 Years of Dance Photography by Frank Capri*

Hall of Fame Inductees:

The New Dance Group

Arthur and Kathryn Murray

Dancer Hall of Fame Inductee:

Frankie Manning

Gala:

Masquerade

Notable:

SPAC forgave the Museum $1.2 million in debt, allowing it to function as a separate entity.

The Art in the Foyer series was instituted.

2007

CLOCKWISE FROM TOP LEFT:
Bob Fosse's Hall of Fame tribute panel.

Dancers and participants in Lawrence
White's *The Moving Figure: A Photography
Workshop.*

Invitation to *Gala Masako,* August 4, 2007.

A view of the exhibition *On Broadway: The
Evolution of Dance on the Broadway Stage.*

A view of the installation in progress of
*Choreo-Motion: A Children's Journey
through Space, Time and Energy.*

Exhibitions:

*On Broadway: The Evolution of
Dance on the Broadway Stage*

*The Dawn of Modern Dance: Music,
Myth and Movement*

Two Dancers—photographs by
Charles Bremer and poetry by Robert
Bensen

Dance Education in America

Dance Across New York

Art in the Foyer:

Paintings by Frank Ohman

Some Dancers I Know—photographs
by Steve Clark

Just Black and White—photographs
by Clifford Oliver

The Art of Movement—photographs
by Rebecca Singer

*The Splendor of Dance in Photo-
graphic Form*—photographs by Catherine Moda

*The Moving Figure: A Photography
Workshop*—by Lawrence White

Hall of Fame Inductees:

Bill T. Jones

Bob Fosse

Gala:

Gala Masako

Notable:

The Mr. and Mrs. Cornelius Vanderbilt
Whitney Hall of Fame was moved to
the south gallery.

*Choreo-Motion: A Children's Journey
through Space, Time and Energy*
opened.

2008

CLOCKWISE FROM TOP LEFT:

A view of the exhibition *Dance Education in America*.

Helmut Huber and Susan Lucci at the *Cirque de Danse* gala, August 2, 2008.

Peter Martins at his Hall of Fame induction, July 14, 2008.

Cartoon featured in *The Daily Gazette*, created by artist Bob Emmons, January 13, 2008.

Exhibitions:

Jerome Robbins Celebration

On Broadway: The Evolution of Dance on the Broadway Stage

Two Dancers—photographs by Charles Bremer and poetry by Robert Bensen

Dance Education in America

Art in the Foyer:

Steele: The Physique of a Dancer and *Smoke in Mirrors*—photographs by Mark Andrew

Hall of Fame Inductee:

Peter Martins

Gala:

Cirque de Danse

Notable:

Donna Skiff was appointed director.

A temporary tribute display was mounted in the Hall of Fame honoring inductee Peter Martins.

2009

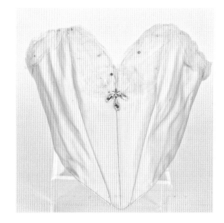

CLOCKWISE FROM TOP LEFT:
Tommy Tune and his sister Gracey Tune at the induction.

Tommy Tune signing lithographs at his Hall of Fame induction, August 2, 2009.

View of the exhibition *Ballets Russes*.

Shaun O'Brien at the *Coppélia 35th Anniversary* celebration, July 15, 2009.

Bodice worn by Darci Kistler, ballet unknown, featured in a display for *A Darci Kistler Tribute*, July 17, 2009. Gift of NYCB.

Exhibitions:

Ballets Russes

Red Shoes–photographs by Kenn Duncan

Washington Bathhouse

Mark Morris Dance Group

On Broadway: The Evolution of Dance on the Broadway Stage

A Tribute to Tommy Tune

Art in the Foyer:

Ballet, Broadway, and Beyond–photographs by Paul Kolnik

Hall of Fame Inductee:

Tommy Tune

Gala:

Gala on Broadway

Notable:

Washington Bathhouse opened as a permanent exhibition in the northeast gallery.

Edward Villella, Suzanne Farrell, Marge Champion, and Frankie Manning were inducted into the Mr. and Mrs. Cornelius Vanderbilt Whitney Hall of Fame after the dissolution of the Dancer Hall of Fame, into which they were each originally inducted.

The small display, *Coppélia 35th Anniversary*, was installed at the Museum to honor the first Balanchine-NYCB work commissioned by SPAC in 1974. A celebration was held on July 15, 2009 with guest of honor Shaun O'Brien, the original Dr. Coppélius.

2010

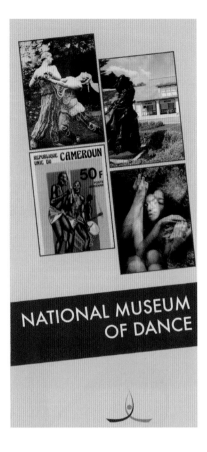

CLOCKWISE FROM TOP LEFT:
A view of the exhibition *Dancing with the Stars*.

Marlon Jackson and Marylou Whitney at the *Tribute to Michael Jackson* gala, August 14, 2010.

The Museum's 2010 season brochure.

A view of the exhibition *Postage Paid: Dance Around the World*.

A view of the *Alfred Z. Solomon Children's Wing*.

Exhibitions:
In a Labyrinth: The Dance of Butoh–photographs by Michael Philip Manheim

Postage Paid: Dance Around the World

MJ: A Michael Jackson Tribute

Dancing with the Stars

Alfred Z. Solomon Children's Wing

Ballets Russes

Art in the Foyer:
Celestial Bodies/Infernal Souls–photographs by Lois Greenfield

Hall of Fame Inductee:
Michael Jackson

Gala:
Tribute to Michael Jackson

Notable:
The Museum received a $20,000 grant from the Alfred Z. Solomon Charitable Trust to create a new, permanent interactive Children's Wing in the north gallery.

The Museum's Resource Room was established and opened to the public.

A small display, *A Midsummer Night's Dream*, was mounted at the Museum to honor the first ballet performed by NYCB at SPAC in its 1966 inaugural season.

Three temporary tribute displays were mounted in the Hall of Fame honoring inductees Bill T. Jones (2007), Arthur and Kathryn Murray (2006), and José Limón (1997).

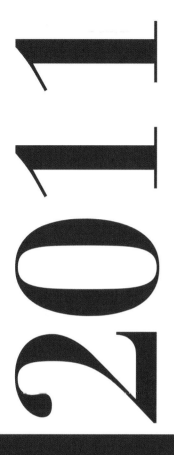

2011

CLOCKWISE FROM TOP LEFT:

The Museum's facility coordinator Shelley Caswell with Ann-Margret at the *Silver Anniversary Gala*, August 6, 2011.

Signage for *Eleo Pomare: The Man, The Artist, The Maker of Artists*.

A view of the exhibition *American Ballet Theatre: Then and Now*.

A view of the tribute display honoring Hall of Fame inductee Trisha Brown.

A view of the tribute display honoring Lifetime Achievement Award recipient Ann-Margret.

Exhibitions:

National Museum of Dance 25th Anniversary Celebration

American Ballet Theatre: Then and Now

Eleo Pomare: The Man, The Artist, The Maker of Artists

Postage Paid: Dance Around the World

Dancing with the Stars

MJ: A Michael Jackson Tribute

Balanchine: a tempo–Paul Kolnik digital exhibition

Art in the Foyer:

Masters of Movement and *From the Wings*–photographs by Rose Eichenbaum

Hall of Fame Inductees:

Frederic Franklin

Oliver Smith

Lifetime Achievement Award:

Ann-Margret

Gala:

Silver Anniversary Gala

Notable:

A small display, *Jewels*, was created by the Museum to honor this work which has been performed by NYCB at SPAC since 1967.

A sustainable garden and fountain were donated and installed at the Museum entrance by Chip's Landscaping and Kohl's Department Store. A Michael Jackson Butterfly Garden was created within this space, underwritten by an anonymous donor.

2012

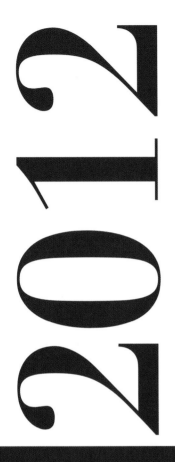

CLOCKWISE FROM TOP LEFT:
Megan Fairchild at an autograph signing.

A view from the exhibition *Tails and Terpsichore* with the Art in the Foyer installation *Christopher Duggan at Inside/ Out: In Celebration of Jacob's Pillow 80th Season* in the background.

A view of pointe shoes in the *En Pointe!* exhibition selected from a pointe shoe decorating contest organized by the Museum.

Invitation to the *Song and Dance* gala.

Flamenco Vivo Carlota Santana performing in the Museum's foyer.

Exhibitions:

En Pointe!

Tails and Terpsichore

American Ballet Theatre: Then and Now

Eleo Pomare: The Man, The Artist, The Maker of Artists

A Tribute to Ben Vereen

Art in the Foyer:

Christopher Duggan at Inside/Out: In Celebration of Jacob's Pillow 80th Season

Hall of Fame Inductee:

Ben Vereen

Gala:

Song and Dance

Notable:

The Museum received an additional $10,000 grant from the Alfred Z. Solomon Trust to further expand and improve the Children's Wing.

The National Museum of Dance Race was inaugurated at the historic Saratoga Race Course on August 18.

The Museum and board president Michele Riggi were honored at the Career Transition for Dancers Gala in October.

Firebird, a mural created by artist Michael Carmen Gentile II, was installed in the Museum for the 2012 season to celebrate the beloved Balanchine-Robbins ballet performed by NYCB at SPAC since 1967.

2013

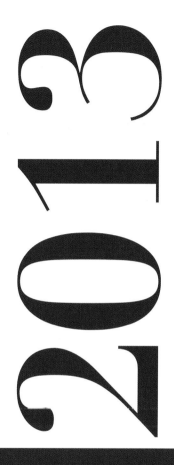

CLOCKWISE FROM TOP LEFT:

An image from the Art in the Foyer exhibition *Dancers Among Us*—photographs by Jordan Matter.

A view of the exhibition *Homage to Dance*—sculpture and drawings by Andrew DeVries.

Brochure for *Saratoga En Pointe*.

A rendering by Tom Frost of the entrance to the newly redesigned Hall of Fame.

The opening reception for the *Saratoga En Pointe* citywide art installation.

Saratoga En Pointe is a community arts project brought to you by the National Museum of Dance.

NATIONAL MUSEUM OF DANCE

Exhibitions:

Homage to Dance—sculpture and drawings by Andrew DeVries

A Riotous Work: A Centennial Celebration of The Rite of Spring

Tails and Terpsichore

En Pointe!

Art in the Foyer:

Dancers Among Us—photographs by Jordan Matter

Hall of Fame Inductees:

Judith Jamison

Anna Pavlova

Gala:

Copacabana

Notable:

The Mr. and Mrs. Cornelius Vanderbilt Whitney Hall of Fame was completely renovated and redesigned, sponsored by Marylou Whitney and John Hendrickson.

Board president Michele Riggi initiated *Saratoga En Pointe*, a citywide art exhibition in which more than thirty, five-foot-tall pointe shoe sculptures were commissioned and painted by local artists to benefit the Museum and highlight Saratoga Springs as a cultural destination.

2014

CLOCKWISE FROM TOP LEFT:

A full-scale paper tutu sculpture *The Firebird: Francesca "Frankie"* by Nicole Battelle Van Hook, displayed in the exhibition *Tiaras and Tutus*. Gift of Nicole Battelle Van Hook.

Invitation to the opera performance *A Night of Love and Jealousy* with tenor Angelo Mazzone, soprano Catherine Mazzone, soprano Roxanne Roweder, and pianist Mun tzung Wong in the Riggi Theater, October 17, 2014.

A view of the exhibition *A Tribute to Gene Kelly*.

The permanent installation *Dancers in Film*.

A view of the exhibition *Dance Theatre of Harlem: 40 Years of Firsts*.

Exhibitions:

Dancers in Film

Dance Theatre of Harlem: 40 Years of Firsts

Tiaras and Tutus

Tradition in Movement: Dance Culture of Guatemala

Saratoga Favorites—dance reviews by Mae Banner and illustrations by Shawn Banner

A Tribute to Jacques d'Amboise

A Tribute to Gene Kelly

Art in the Foyer:

Dance Magic: The Photography of Richard Calmes

Hall of Fame Inductees:

Jacques d'Amboise

Gene Kelly

Lifetime Achievement Award:

John Travolta

Gala:

Dancers in Film

Notable:

Raul P. Martinez was appointed director.

The Mr. and Mrs. Ronald A. Riggi Theater opened on July 24.

The Museum was awarded a $14,000 grant from The Highland Kansas City Foundation, Inc. through John Honis of Highland Capital Management for the purchase of touch screen technology in the Hall of Fame.

The Museum received two important bronze sculptures, *Dancing Group* and *Ballet Dancers*, created by world-renowned twentieth-century artist George Gách, a gift from his grandson Beau R. Peelle.

2015

NATIONAL MUSEUM OF DANCE

2015 Season

CLOCKWISE FROM TOP LEFT:
Diane Lachtrupp and Johnny Martinez of Tango Fusion performing at the opening of *125 Years of Tango: A Walk through the History of the Dance*, March 21, 2015.

Cast members of Dancing with the Stars from left, Sasha Farber, Valentin Chmerkovskiy, Brittany Cherry, and Emma Slater at a meet and greet at the Museum, June 14, 2015.

The Museum's 2015 season brochure.

The second annual Move and Groove 5K hosted by the Museum.

Exhibitions:
Making Art Dance—Karole Armitage

125 Years of Tango: A Walk through the History of the Dance

A Tribute to Mark Morris

A Tribute to Rudolf Nureyev

Saratoga Favorites—dance reviews by Mae Banner and illustrations by Shawn Banner

Art in the Foyer:
The Cris Alexander and Shaun O'Brien Collection

Hall of Fame Inductees:
Mark Morris

Rudolf Nureyev

Lifetime Achievement Award:
Chita Rivera

Gala:
¡Tango!

Notable:
The Museum received a $5,000 grant from the Rudolf Nureyev Dance Foundation, in addition to a pair of ballet shoes worn by Nureyev, in honor of his induction into the Hall of Fame.

2016

CLOCKWISE FROM TOP LEFT:

Artist Alice Manzi and Museum director Raul P. Martinez at the opening reception for Manzi's nine-piece sculpture *Gen*.

A view of the exhibition *50 Years at SPAC*.

Museum staff with Hall of Fame inductee Patricia Wilde at her meet and greet, August 15, 2016, standing from left, Jessica Munson, Shelley Caswell, Raul P. Martinez, Laura DiRado, Nina Garay, and Lisa Schlansker Kolosek, seated from left, Mary Anne Fantauzzi and Patricia Wilde.

A view of the installation in progress of *The Dancing Athlete*.

Asian Culture Chinese Dance performing in the Museum foyer on Multicultural Dance Day, October 16, 2016.

Exhibitions:

The Dancing Athlete

50 Years at SPAC

A Tribute to Patricia Wilde

A Tribute to Gregory Hines

Saratoga Favorites—dance reviews by Mae Banner and illustrations by Shawn Banner

Gen—Alice Manzi—outdoor exhibition

Art in the Foyer:

Moment to Moment: A History of Time and Place—photographs by Paul Kolnik

Hall of Fame Inductees:

Patricia Wilde

Gregory Hines

Gala:

The Dancing Athlete

2017

CLOCKWISE FROM TOP LEFT:
Frozen Dance Party, February 2017.

Kim Vanyo of Khymanyo Studio walking the runway at the finish of her fashion show at Arts Fest Friday Gotta Dance!, hosted by the Museum, March 31, 2017.

Costume design from the Khymanyo Studio fashion show at the Museum, March 31, 2017.

Dancers and participants in Lawrence White's Photo Fusion photography class, April 2017.

The Museum's 30th Anniversary logo.

Exhibitions:

National Museum of Dance: Celebrating 30 Years

Mr. and Mrs. Cornelius Vanderbilt Whitney Hall of Fame: Celebrating the Founders

The Dancing Athlete

Gen—Alice Manzi—outdoor exhibition

Art in the Foyer:

Design for Dance: The Malcolm McCormick Collection

Hall of Fame Inductees:

Marylou Whitney

Lewis A. Swyer

Gala:

30th Anniversary Pearl Gala

Notable:

The National Museum of Dance and Hall of Fame: Celebrating 30 Years, by Lisa Schlansker Kolosek, was published by the State University of New York Press, supported by a grant from the J.M. Kaplan Fund.

Michele Riggi

President, National Museum of Dance and Hall of Fame

From the moment when I first walked through the doors of this beautiful building, it was clear that the National Museum of Dance and Hall of Fame was nothing short of a cultural jewel. Not only is it an architectural and historical treasure, but it is the only museum in this country where the art form of dance is honored and truly lives. Now in my twelfth year as President of the Board of Directors, it continues to be an absolute privilege to serve the Museum in this capacity. And my original vision is still very clear – to keep dreaming of how we can make this wonderful place even better. Each year we strive to create greater national and international awareness of our institution through our increasingly innovative exhibitions and programming. The growth of the School of the Arts is one of my main priorities, and with that the continued expansion of the curriculum to offer arts education in all facets of the performing arts. We hope to build on our founding mission of presenting live dance to the community through increased master classes, lecture-demonstrations, and performances, and we plan to utilize our unique outdoor space to even greater advantage for this purpose. At this thrilling milestone for the National Museum of Dance I ask you to join us in celebrating, promoting, and most especially supporting this very essential art form and my lifelong passion - dance!

FACING PAGE:
President of the board Michele Riggi with students from the School of the Arts, from left, Hanna Heneghan, Ella Sampson, William Halm, Alexandra Nicolaus, Sarah MacGregor, Lilah DuBoff, Cordelia Padovan, and Ellery DuBoff.

ACKNOWLEDGEMENTS

I would first like to thank Michele and Ron Riggi for their extraordinary dedication to and support of the National Museum of Dance, and the Board of Directors including Safwat Gerges, Eileen Guarino, Mario Martinez, Carol Swyer, and John Witt for their generous support of this project.

My sincere thanks go to Raul P. Martinez for the opportunity to write this book, his inspiring vision for the Museum, and his sound leadership. Thank you to Laura DiRado, whose ingenious design always makes my words look so much better, and this book is certainly no exception. I am truly grateful for her expert management of this project and her constant encouragement. I share this accomplishment in equal measure with her. I thank Jessica Munson for her critical research assistance and attention to detail, as well as the great sense of morale she always brings to the table. Erik Stolarski was essential to my research and to understanding the collection and archive, I could not have done this without his collaboration. It is a pleasure to be in the company each day of Jo Ambrosio, Shelley Caswell, and Lindsey Carney who round out the Museum team and add to the magic of this place.

Enormous thanks go to Mark Morris for his outstanding foreword and to Nancy Umanoff for her support. Thank you to Karole Armitage, Andrew DeVries, and Paul Kolnik for their advance review of the book and their kind words.

I thank Marylou Whitney and John Hendrickson for their time and interest in this project, and Edward and Carol Swyer for sharing the personal papers of their father, Lewis A. Swyer, and for their incredible generosity of time. Thank you to founding board member Nancy Norman Lassalle for her vital historical insight.

The past thirty years of the Museum truly came alive for me through conversations with many key individuals from the Museum's past and present. I must first thank Mary Anne Fantauzzi, volunteer from the very beginning, who loaned us thirty years of docent files and who made herself available for hours upon hours of conversation about the Museum and innumerable inquiries via text and email. The Museum is so lucky to have her in its corner. Carolyn Adams, Siobhan Dunham, and Susan Edwards also made themselves infinitely available for questions and conversation and were essential to my understanding of the history of the Museum, many thanks. And equally to Heather Mabee, Sharon Walsh, and Judi Fiore for their time and valuable perspectives. Former directors Alison Moore, Joanne Allison, Maurice O'Connell, Beth Hartle Fecteau, and Donna Skiff were also tremendously helpful and generous in articulating the development and evolution of the Museum. Guest curators Denise Limoli and Leslie Roy-Heck were critical in identifying numerous collection pieces, as was the unwavering assistance and interest of longtime curator Norton Owen and the generosity of designer Kevan Moss. My thanks also go to Connie Frisbee Houde, the Saratoga Room at the Saratoga Springs Public Library, and the Saratoga Springs New York State Office of Parks, Recreation, and Historic Preservation for their help in my research.

Many of the photographs in this book were taken by Lisa Miller of Studio di Luce, as well as photographer Lawrence White. I thank them both for their time and generosity. I would also like to thank Larry Abrams, Mark Bolles, Steven Caras, Marguerite Hill, Imagine! Photography and Design, Paul Kolnik, and Joe Putrock for their time spent searching their archives and for so generously allowing us to include their photographs in the book.

For RVS, to and for whom I am eternally grateful.

ENDNOTES

CHAPTER ONE:

[1] Since the mid1980s, three additional NYCB works have received world premieres at SPAC, including two by its resident choreographer, Justin Peck.

[2] Sally Sears Mack, "Saratoga School of Modern Dance: Chapter One in a Dream Come True," *Dance Magazine* (July 1970): 40-41.

[3] Oleg Briansky and Mireille Briane donated a collection of photographs and artifacts from their careers and school to the Museum in 2016.

[4] Denise Warner Limoli, *Dance in Saratoga Springs* (Charleston: The History Press, 2013), 26-28.

[5] State of New York Saratoga Springs Commission, *The Medicinal Waters and Baths at Saratoga Springs* (Albany: J. B. Lyon Company, Printers, 1934), 5.

[6] National Dance Hall of Fame, Inc., *ByLaws of The National Dance Hall of Fame, Inc.* (1984), 1.

[7] In 1988, the Museum received a $100,000 grant from the Samuel Freeman Charitable Trust for the reconstruction of the northeast wing as well as for additional gallery and exhibition storage facilities.

[8] *National Museum of Dance: Fact Sheet* (July 8, 1986), 2.

[9] National Dance Hall of Fame, Inc., *Proposal for the Acquisition and ReUse of the Washington Bathhouse* (1984), 1. From 1990 to 2006, the Museum was a program of SPAC.

[10] In 2009, Lassalle became an honorary board member and remains so to this day.

[11] Heather Mabee, Marylou Whitney's daughter, was on the board for several years including six years as president. Edward and Carol Swyer, Lewis A. Swyer's son and daughter, have represented the Swyer family on the board since his death in 1988 and continue to do so.

[12] A recipient of *Forbes* magazine's National Business in the Arts Award and the New York State Governor's Arts Award, one of the two theaters in The Egg Center for the Performing Arts at the Empire State Plaza in Albany is named in Swyer's honor. The other theater at The Egg is named in honor of Kitty Carlisle Hart.

[13] Interview with Edward Swyer, February 2, 2017.

[14] Letter from Lewis A. Swyer to Marylou Whitney, September 16, 1987, Lewis A. Swyer Papers, National Museum of Dance and Hall of Fame.

[15] This fountain and one located on the front southeast terrace were decommissioned.

[16] Interview with Alison Moore, December 8, 2016.

[17] Interview with Alison Moore, February 9, 2017.

[18] "Judith Brown, 60, Figurative Sculptor; Worked in Metals," *The New York Times* (May 15, 1992).

[19] "Bringing up the rear…," *New York Post* (June 6, 1986): 61.

[20] Mary-Jane Tichenor, "Horsey set reigns at Saratoga. Museum gala opens season," *Berkshire Eagle* (August 12, 1986): 17-18.

[21] The National Museum of Dance opened thirty years to the day after SPAC.

[22] Elizabeth Ellsworth, "The Museum that Jack Built," *Nutshell News* (July 1988): 54-56.

[23] The volunteers, in particular, provided a level of energy and enthusiasm that helped to sustain the morale and function of the Museum through its most challenging years. Over its thirty-year history, the Museum has at times experienced acute financial uncertainty and a frequent turnover of directors.

CHAPTER TWO:

[1] Leslie Roy-Heck is also the founder of Saratoga Dance Etc.

[2] Bill Bradley is credited with creating the Gypsy Robe, a historic symbol of good luck in which the chorus member with the most Broadway credits receives a robe on a show's opening night containing mementos from the shows of former recipients of the robe. This tradition has been in place since 1949 and continues to this day.

[3] This exhibition was extended for a second year and moved from its original placement within the Museum to the foyer for the 2002 season.

[4] Interview with former director Beth Hartle, November 17, 2016.

[5] *Moment to Moment: A History of Time and Place* was mounted for the 2016 season and chronicled NYCB at SPAC. The exhibition was created in celebration of SPAC's fiftieth anniversary.

[6] Nancy Norman Lassalle was involved with *Ballet for a City and a Nation: Forty Years of the New York City Ballet* (1988), *Balanchine: A Celebration of His Work* (1993), *Firebird and the New York City Ballet 1949-1995* (1995), *New York City Ballet: Our Time in Saratoga Springs* (1999), and *The Enduring Legacy of George Balanchine* (2004). Bigelow co-curated the 1988, 1995, and 1999 exhibitions with her. Madeleine Nichols and Susan Au co-curated the 1993 exhibition. Nichols also co-curated the 2004 exhibition.

[7] "Present day" meaning the year of the exhibition, 1995.

[8] Jeannette Jordan, "'Firebird' comes alive," *The Saratogian* (July 22, 1995).

[9] Anna Kisselgoff, "Taking Fresh Stock of Les Ballets 1933," *The New York Times* (August 19, 1990).

[10] Nancy Norman Lassalle facilitated the loan of the exhibition, which she had collaborated on when it was first presented in England. Lassalle also served as editor of the Museum catalog for this show.

[11] Anna Sokolow was inducted into the Hall of Fame in 1998 and an exhibition in her honor, *Anna Sokolow: The Rebellious Spirit*, was curated by Norton Owen and designed by Kevan Moss. *Dancers of Limón: Photographs of Susan Rubin* was also on view in the 1998 season.

[12] The Museum consulted with Genevieve Oswald, the founding curator of the Dance Division at the New York Public Library, in advance of its 1986 opening. Oswald accepted the Hall of Fame award for Catherine Littlefield at her induction on July 11, 1987, just two months before her retirement from the New York Public Library.

[13] Wendy Liberatore, "Innovative New Dance Group inducted into Hall of Fame," *The Daily Gazette* (August 13, 2006), B1 and B3.

[14] Other exhibitions at the Museum that have honored cultural dance forms include *Dance of the Iroquois* (2006), *In a Labyrinth: The Dance of Butoh* (2010), and *Tradition in Movement: Dance Culture of Guatemala* (2014).

[15] Veteran MOMIX dancer, Brian Simerson, whose 2012 dance work *Bach and Forth* is highlighted in *The Dancing Athlete*, choreographed and performed a new sports-inspired work, *Metamorphosis*, for the exhibition opening on April 23, 2016. Joan K. Anderson choreographed a baseball-inspired dance work, *The Old Ballgame*, for students at the Museum's School of the Arts that was performed at *The Dancing Athlete* gala on August 13, 2016.

[16] Lewis A. Swyer opening remarks, Mr. and Mrs. Cornelius Vanderbilt Whitney Hall of Fame Induction Ceremony, July 11, 1987.

[17] Frances Ingraham, "Dance Inductees Honored in NYC at Vanderbilt Penthouse," *Times Union* (June 7, 1987), B-2.

[18] Hope Hawthorne, mother of former New York City Ballet soloist Robert Maiorano, created her stained glass Hall of Fame award for seven inductees between 1989 and 1998. Hawthorne also enjoyed commissions for stained glass windows from Lincoln Kirstein for his carriage house in Manhattan and his home in Westport, Connecticut, over the course of twenty years.

[19] Katherine Dunham acceptance speech, Mr. and Mrs. Cornelius Vanderbilt Whitney Hall of Fame Induction Ceremony, July 11, 1987.

[20] In 2004, a new Hall of Fame category was created, Dancer's Hall of Fame, into which Marge Champion, Suzanne Farrell, and Edward Villella were inducted that year, and Frankie Manning in 2006. In 2009, the Museum decided to discontinue this category and inducted Champion, Farrell, Manning, and Villella into the existing Hall of Fame. In 2011, the first Lifetime Achievement Award was presented to Ann-Margret. This award has subsequently been presented to John Travolta in 2014 and Chita Rivera in 2015.

[21] Warhol's *Silver Clouds* is an installation of free-floating silver Mylar helium-filled balloons. Cunningham used this installation as part of his 1968 dance work *RainForest*.

22 Kevan Moss Design was also responsible for the installation and design of *Body and Soul: The Alvin Ailey American Dance Theater* (1992) and *New York City Ballet: Our Time in Saratoga Springs* (1999).

23 Mark Morris acceptance speech, Mr. and Mrs. Cornelius Vanderbilt Whitney Hall of Fame Induction Ceremony, *¡Tango!* Gala, August 8, 2015. The Museum presented a smaller exhibition honoring Mark Morris Dance Group in 2009, on the occasion of Mark Morris Dance Group's performance at SPAC.

CHAPTER THREE:

1 National Dance Hall of Fame, Inc., *Proposal for the Acquisition and Re-Use of the Washington Bathhouse* (1984).

2 Rudolf Nureyev was inducted into the Hall of Fame in 2015. Barry L. Weinstein, president of the Rudolf Nureyev Dance Foundation, accepted the award at the August 8, 2015, gala and induction ceremony. In honor of this occasion, the Museum received one of the last grants given by the Foundation, in addition to a pair of Nureyev's ballet shoes.

3 In 1963, *Sets in Order* magazine became *Square Dancing* magazine.

4 Oliver Smith's first professional scenic design was for Léonide Massine's *Saratoga*, commissioned by the Ballet Russe de Monte Carlo.

5 Lois Doherty-Mander accepted Lucia Chase's Hall of Fame award at the July 9, 1988, induction ceremony on behalf of Chase's son, Alex C. Ewing.

6 McCormick is the coauthor, with Nancy Reynolds, of the award-winning *No Fixed Points: Dance in the Twentieth Century* (2003).

7 John Hay Whitney was a first cousin to Cornelius Vanderbilt Whitney. Their lives were intertwined in many respects including thoroughbred horse breeding and racing, summers in Saratoga Springs, and a successful business partnership in Hollywood.

8 This exhibition was designed by Kevan Moss of Kevan Moss Design and curated by Norton Owen, director of preservation at Jacob's Pillow.

9 The Olympiad costume is on temporary loan from Jacob's Pillow. Dreier co-founded the Société Anonyme, an organization created to promote and support modern art and emerging artists, in 1920 with Marcel Duchamp and Man Ray.

10 *A Dreier Lithograph* was also presented by the Carol Lynn Ballet at the Baltimore Museum of Art in January 1939. Lynn worked with Shawn as associate director of Jacob's Pillow from 1943 to 1960. Robin Veder, *The Living Line: Modern Art and the Economy of Energy* (Lebanon, NH: University Press of New England, 2015), 281.

11 Photographer Paul Kolnik has presented two digital displays at the Museum, in 2011 and 2016, of his documentation of NYCB. The 2016 Art in the Foyer exhibition, *Moment to Moment: A History of Time and Place*, featured Kolnik's images of NYCB at SPAC over the course of the past forty years.

12 At his induction ceremony, Tommy Tune signed copies of his lithographs of which one hundred percent of the proceeds were donated to the Museum. Nicole Flender, "And…They're Off!," *Equity News* (September 2009).

13 *The Fugitive Gesture: Masterpieces of Dance Photography 1849 to the Present* was drawn from Ewing's 1987 book of the same title.

14 Kolnik's two digital displays were *Balanchine: a tempo* in 2011 and a supplement to *Moment to Moment: A History of Time and Place* installed within the Museum's 2016 exhibition, *50 Years at SPAC*.

CHAPTER FOUR:

1 The construction of the studios was initially intended as the third and final phase of the three-phase plan of the establishment of the National Museum of Dance. However, with the completion of the studios in 1992 it became the second major phase realized. The original plan called for the construction of a theater within the Museum as a centerpiece of phase two. The completion of the Mr. and Mrs. Ronald A. Riggi Theater in 2014 ultimately fulfilled the founding vision.

2 Ray Rinaldi, "Ground Broken for Swyer School of Dance," *The Times Union* (November 21, 1991), B15.

3 Bill Rice, "Dance Museum Breaks Ground for Swyer School," *The Daily Gazette* (November 21, 1991).

4 William E. Murray also served as the longtime chairman of the Samuel Freeman Trust. "William E. Murray†, Position: Director Emeritus," https://www.eastwest.ngo/profile/william-e-murray-†.

5 Interview with Edward Swyer, February 2, 2017.

6 Letter from Michael D. Bart, Attorney at Law, to the Director of the National Museum of Dance, December 30, 1992, Hanya Holm Collection, National Museum of Dance and Hall of Fame.

7 Marilyn Storz, "Windows on the World: The Lewis A. Swyer School for the Performing Arts," *New York City Ballet News* (Fall 1992).

8 Saratoga Performing Arts Center, "SPAC Builds Dance Studios to House New York State Summer School of the Arts' Schools of Ballet and Dance," news release, November 20, 1991.

9 Bill Rice, "Dance Museum Breaks Ground for Swyer School."

10 The original folding wall system was replaced with an updated folding wall system in 2011.

11 All NYSSSA students are housed at Skidmore College during their residencies and certain classes are taught at the Skidmore College Dance Theater.

12 Philip Seymour Hoffman and John Ortiz were the coartistic directors of the Labyrinth Theater at the time of its residency at the Swyer Studios. Saratoga Stages was founded and directed by Bruce Bouchard, and in 2002 considered the Studios its temporary home base.

13 This successful program was led for ten years by writer and dance enthusiast Marilyn Rothstein, known in the literary world as M. E. Kemp.

14 Figures in Flight 5 was established by choreographer Susan Slotnick under the auspices of New York State Rehabilitation Through the Arts. When this special event was presented at the Museum, it was the only program of its kind in a men's prison in the United States and one of only a few in the world.

15 *An Evening in Old Saratoga* was organized for the National Museum of Dance in 1986 by the not-for-profit corporation An Evening in Old Saratoga, Inc, chaired by Beverly Ensor. Beginning in 1987, the Museum produced their own galas.

16 Fred Ferretti, "Social Season in Saratoga Springs Hits Its Stride," *The New York Times* (August 8, 1984).

17 Frances Ingraham, "Parties Focus on Museum of Dance," *The Times Union* (August 12, 1987).

18 Barry Schwartz is also the co-founder and chairman of Calvin Klein, Inc.

19 The four Whitney galas at the Canfield Casino that benefited the Museum were *Saratoga Trunk* (1990), *Silver Buck* (1997), *The Phantom of the Opera* (1998), and *Showboat* (1999).

20 Rudolf Nureyev staged the first three-act version of *La Bayadère* for the Paris Opera Ballet in October 1992, the final work of his career before his death on January 6, 1993.

21 Jeannette Jordan, "Dance Gala Hard Act to Follow," *The Times Union* (August 1994).

22 Bill Cunningham, "Homage to two Nureyevs. Benefit for the National Museum of Dance, Saratoga Springs, N.Y., Aug. 6," *The New York Times* (August 14, 1994).

23 As part of his 2009 gala performance, Tommy Tune also performed with his sister Gracey Tune and Museum president Michele Riggi.

24 The Museum lost power on the night of *The Dancing Athlete*, August 13, 2016.

PHOTO CREDITS

Every reasonable attempt has been made to identify owners of copyright. Errors or omissions should be brought to the attention of the publisher and will be corrected in subsequent printings. Any photographs not credited here are in the public domain.

Foreword, Introduction, Chapter One: ii: Saratoga Springs, New York State Office of Parks, Recreation, and Historic Preservation. vi: Saratoga Springs, New York State Office of Parks, Recreation, and Historic Preservation. viii: Amber Star Merkens. x: Imagine! Photography and Design. xii: Saratoga Illustrated. 3: Left and right, ©Paul Kolnik. Courtesy Paul Kolnik. BALANCHINE is a Trademark of The George Balanchine Trust. 4: Bob Mayette, Briansky Collection, National Museum of Dance. 5: Left, ©Paul Kolnik. Courtesy Paul Kolnik. BALANCHINE is a Trademark of The George Balanchine Trust. 6: George S. Bolster Collection of the Historical Society of Saratoga Springs. 7-9: Saratoga Springs, New York State Office of Parks, Recreation, and Historic Preservation. 10: Saratoga Illustrated. 11: Right, Saratoga Illustrated. 12: Top left, Bert and Richard Morgan Photographers; bottom right, Christopher P. Collins. 13: Imagine! Photography and Design. 18: Lisa Miller, Studio di Luce. 19: Raul Martinez. 20: David Wells, *NY Daily News*. 23: Left: Phil Haggerty; right, Mort Kaye Studios, Inc.

Chapter Two: 28: Daesha Devón Harris. 30: Top, Daesha Devón Harris. 31: Imagine! Photography and Design. 32: Imagine! Photography and Design. 33: Top, Lisa Miller, Studio di Luce; bottom middle and right, Imagine! Photography and Design. 36: Lawrence White. 37: Cris Alexander. 39: Top left and right, ©Paul Kolnik. Courtesy Paul Kolnik; bottom left and right, Lisa Miller, Studio di Luce. 40: Top, Laura DiRado. 41: Laura DiRado. 44: Center, Lisa Miller, Studio di Luce. 45: Right top and bottom, Lisa Miller, Studio di Luce. 46: Lisa Miller, Studio di Luce. 47: Walter E. Owen. 48: Left top and bottom, Donna Eichmeyer. 50: Raoul Barba, Monte Carlo. 52: Center, George Hoyningen-Huene, Kurt Weill Foundation for Music, New York, right, Janet Jevons, Rambert Dance Company Archive. 53: Left and right, Boris Lipnitzki, Roger-Viollet archive, Paris. 60: Ed Burke, *The Saratogian*. 61: Left, Lisa Miller, Studio di Luce; right top, Lisa Miller, Studio di Luce. 62: Jack B. Mitchell. 63: Collection of Doris Jones. 64: Left, Peter Basch, Dance Collection, John Linquist, Jacob's Pillow Archive; right, Jack B. Mitchell. 65: Jack B. Mitchell. 68: Top left, Carolyn Adams. 70: Lisa Miller, Studio di Luce. 71: Lisa Miller, Studio di Luce. 72: Top left, Laura DiRado; all others, Lisa Miller, Studio di Luce. 73: Left, Lisa Miller, Studio di Luce; top right, Imagine! Photography and Design; bottom right, Jessica Munson. 74-76: Lisa Miller, Studio di Luce. 77: Left, Lisa Miller, Studio di Luce; top right, Colleen Dunphy Zorbas; bottom right, Lisa Miller, Studio di Luce. 78: Left top and bottom, Lisa Miller, Studio di Luce; right, Colleen Dunphy Zorbas. 79: Lawrence White. 82: Left top, S. Rucker; center top and bottom, Lisa Miller, Studio di Luce; right, Lisa Miller, Studio di Luce. 83: Lisa Miller, Studio di Luce. 84: All photos, S. Rucker. 85: Left, top right, Larry Abrams; center, Christopher Collins; center left, Leif Zurmuhlen; left bottom, Imagine! Photography and Design; right top Lisa Miller, Studio di Luce; right bottom, Jessica Munson. 86: Left and right bottom, Imagine! Photography and Design. 87: Tom Sullivan. 88: Photographer Courtney Frisse/Photo courtesy of Kevan Moss Design. 89: Bottom, Photographer Courtney Frisse/Photo courtesy of Kevan Moss Design. 92: Right top and center bottom, Imagine! Photography and Design; right bottom Daesha Devón Harris. 93: Top, Imagine! Photography and Design; bottom, Daesha Devón Harris. 94: Larry Abrams. 95: Bottom left and right, Donna Eichmeyer. 97: Clockwise from top left, Donna Eichmeyer; Donna Eichmeyer; Photo courtesy of Kevan Moss Design; Photo courtesy of Kevan Moss Design; Photo courtesy of Kevan Moss Design; Donna Eichmeyer. 98: Lisa Miller, Studio di Luce. 99: Left top, Raul Martinez; right top and bottom, Lisa Miller, Studio di Luce.

Chapter Three: All photos in chapter 3, Lisa Miller, Studio di Luce; with the exception of the following: 102: Clockwise from top left, National Museum of Dance Collection, Heidi Vosseler Collection, scrapbooks, 2017. 104: Right bottom, Raul Martinez. 105: Left bottom, Nicholson, Kansas City. 106: Left top, photo provided by Sloans & Kenyon. 107: Top second from left, Raul Martinez. 108: Jessica Munson. 109: E. Lee Smith, courtesy of Mana Contemporary. 110: Top and left and center bottom, E. Lee Smith, courtesy of Mana Contemporary; bottom right, Jessica Munson. 111: Clockwise from top left, Raul Martinez; Raul Martinez; Jessica Munson; Raul Martinez; Jessica Munson; E. Lee Smith, courtesy of Mana Contemporary. 112: Cris Alexander. 113: Left and right, Cris Alexander. 114: All photos, Cris Alexander. 116: Top Right, Cris Alexander. 117: Cris Alexander. 121: Bottom left, Kenn Duncan. 136-139: Gift of Steven Caras, 2017, ©Steven Caras, all rights reserved. 140: Erik Stolarski. 141: Foto Dekkinga, Holland. 145: Jack B. Mitchell. 147: Top right, Shapiro Studio. 151: Right, Raul Martinez. 158: Susan Blackburn. 160: Left photos, Susan Blackburn . 161: Susan Blackburn. 162: ©Walker Evans Archive, The Metropolitan Museum of Art. 163: George Platt Lynes. 164: Laura DiRado. 165: Raul Martinez. 170-172: ©Paul Kolnik. Courtesy Paul Kolnik. 173: ©Paul Kolnik. Courtesy Paul Kolnik. ©The George Balanchine Trust.

Chapter Four: 174: Lawrence White. 177: Bert and Richard Morgan Photographers. 178: Left and right, Lisa Miller, Studio di Luce. 179: Cecil Beaton. 180: Lawrence White. 181: Top, Raul Martinez; bottom left Lawrence White; bottom right, Christie Handley. 190: Lisa Miller, Studio di Luce. 192: Top right, Lisa Miller, Studio di Luce; bottom left and right, Raul Martinez. 193: Clockwise from top left, Alice Corey; Shana ParkeHarrison; Lisa Miller, Studio di Luce; Lisa Miller, Studio di Luce; Moscelyne ParkeHarrison; Lisa Miller, Studio di Luce; Alice Corey. 194: All photos, Lisa Miller, Studio di Luce. 195: Top right, Laura DiRado; all others, Lisa Miller, Studio di Luce. 196-199: Carolyn Adams. 200-201: Raul Martinez. 202-203: Gary David Gold, courtesy of Opera Saratoga. 204-205: All photos, Lawrence White. 206: Raul Martinez . 207: All photos, Lawrence White. 208-209: All photos, Lawrence White. 210: Left, Raul Martinez; right, Lawrence White. 211: All photos, Larry Abrams. 212: Lawrence White. 213: Top left, Raul Martinez; top right and bottom left, Lawrence White. 214: Lawrence White. 215: Anthony G. Tassarotti. 216: Jessica Munson. 217: Bottom left and bottom center, Anthony G. Tassarotti. 218: Top left, Jessica Munson. 220: Left top and bottom and right bottom, Raul Martinez. 222: Bottom left, Raul Martinez; bottom right, Jessica Munson. 224-225: All photos, Raul Martinez. 229: Left top and bottom right, Bert and Richard Morgan Photographers; right bottom left and right, Marguerite Hill. 230: Right, Bert and Richard Morgan Photographers. 232: Left top and bottom, Imagine! Photography and Design; right, Joe Putrock. 233: Imagine! Photography and Design. 234: Left, Joe Putrock; right, Imagine! Photography and Design. 235: Joe Putrock.

Chapter Five: 236: Saratoga Springs, New York State Office of Parks, Recreation, and Historic Preservation. 238: Top left, Saratoga Illustrated. 239: Top middle, S. Rucker. 242: Top left, Lawrence White. 244: Top left, Larry Abrams; center bottom, Photographer Courtney Frisse/Photo courtesy of Kevan Moss Design. 245: Top middle, Lisa Miller, Studio di Luce. 248: Far right, Lisa Miller, Studio di Luce. 249: ©1994 William Boorstein/Boorstein.com. 250: Top left, Marguerite Hill; . 251: Right top, Ed Burke *The Saratogian*. 252: Top row, Marguerite Hill; bottom right, Tom Sullivan. 253: Top left, Siobhan Dunham; top center, ©Steven Caras, all rights reserved; top right, Leif Zurmuhlen. 256: Top middle, Raul Martinez. 258: Top left, Imagine! Photography and Design; bottom right, Lawrence White. 259: Top middle, Lawrence White. 260: Top left, Raul Martinez; top center Imagine! Photography and Design; top right, Raul Martinez; bottom right, Bob Emmons/*The Daily Gazette*. 261: Top row, Raul Martinez; bottom left, Lisa Miller, Studio di Luce. 262: Top center, Imagine! Photography and Design. 263: Top left, Imagine! Photography and Design; top right, Raul Martinez. 265: Top left, Jordan Matter; top center, Daesha Devón Harris; middle center, Imagine! Photography and Design; bottom center, Tom Frost. 266: Top left, Laura DiRado; top right and bottom right, Imagine! Photography and Design; bottom center, Dave Feiden. 267: Top left, Lisa Miller, Studio di Luce; top center and bottom, Jessica Munson. 268: Top row and bottom left, Lisa Miller, Studio di Luce; bottom right, Laura DiRado. 269: Top left, Laura DiRado; top center and top right, TM Williams; bottom right, Lawrence White. 270: Lawrence White. 272: Laura DiRado.

Inside Front and Back Cover: Lawrence White.